DREAMS
DON'T HAVE DEADLINES

DREAMS

DON'T HAVE DEADLINES

LIVING YOUR DREAM LIFE,
NO MATTER WHAT YOUR AGE

MARK VICTOR HANSEN

AN OFFICIAL NIGHTINGALE-CONANT PUBLICATION

Published and distributed by:
SOUND WISDOM
P.O. Box 310
Shippensburg, PA 17257-0310
717-530-2122

info@soundwisdom.com
www.soundwisdom.com

While efforts have been made to verify information contained in this publication, neither the author nor the publisher assumes any responsibility for errors, inaccuracies, or omissions. While this publication is chock-full of useful, practical information; it is not intended to be legal or accounting advice. All readers are advised to seek competent lawyers and accountants to follow laws and regulations that may apply to specific situations. The reader of this publication assumes responsibility for the use of the information. The author and publisher assume no responsibility or liability whatsoever on the behalf of the reader of this publication.

This book contains information that is intended to help the readers be better informed in dealing with change and the challenges it brings to life. It is presented as general advice using the author's experience and best judgment but is in no way to be considered a substitute for necessary care provided by a physician or other medical professional.

ISBN 13 TP: 978-1-64095-098-6
ISBN 13 eBook: 978-1-64095-099-3

For Worldwide Distribution, Printed in the U.S.A.
1 2 3 4 5 6 7 8 / 24 23 22 21 20

CONTENTS

INTRODUCTION

Right now, imagine your life exactly as you want it to be.

What would it take to make you ecstatically happy, totally fulfilled, and 100 percent elated to be alive?

How would you like to just smash the time clock of your life?

How would you like to make the *rest* of your life the *best* of your life?

How would you like to live the life you've always dreamed of?

No one knows more about making dreams come true than Mark Victor Hansen co-creator of the hugely successful *Chicken Soup for the Soul* series. Mark is responsible for the sale of more than 500 million books worldwide with the numbers rising every day. Yet Mark did not achieve anything close to this level of success until he was well into his 40s. How did he finally do it? He knew that dreams don't have any deadlines—and once you've read this exciting and inspiring book, you'll know it too.

As Mark explains, we all started out with big dreams. We imagined the great things we wanted to accomplish for ourselves and for the world. But more often than not, the demands of life in the real world cause us to turn aside from our youthful ambitions. And all too often, those ambitions are forgotten forever. The truth is, this does not have to be so.

What's more, with 75 million Americans now passing the age of 50, our society cannot afford to have this huge segment of the population simply going fishing. For everyone's benefit, we need to take the deadlines off our dreams and start transforming them into the realities of our everyday lives. When that happens, everyone comes out ahead and this book shows how to make it happen. Starting now.

Here are just some of the ideas Mark shares with you throughout the book:

- The importance of multiplicity in goal setting with real-life examples of exactly how it works.

- How to stay connected with people who can help you succeed and how to get connected with people who can help you even more.

- The three basic components of good health, plus the recent innovations that you must understand in order to be at your best.

- Having a mentor is important regardless of your age and why being a mentor is absolutely essential.

- The power of forming a mastermind group.

- Why there's never been a better time to start living your dreams—and why our whole society needs you to do so.

- And so much more.

People from all walks of life—business, music, theatre, coaching, and sports—are now making it big in what people used to call the "second half of life." Yet there's no need for a second half of life while you're still in the first half. It's a well-known fact that people are living much longer today than those of the generations behind them. As Mark puts it, "Dreams don't have deadlines. It's my story; it's your story; it's our story—because no dream has a time limit unless you attach one to it."

And if you haven't achieved your dream at this point in your life, the secret is not to limit it or abandon it but to *renew* it and *expand* it. You can do that, and it requires nothing more than real desire and deep commitment. Once those two key elements are in place, your life takes off in new and exciting directions—and your once-distant future becomes your new reality.

Learn the tools, techniques, strategies, and tactics to live the life you know you were meant to live. It's all in *Dreams Don't Have Deadlines.*

CHAPTER 1

ARE YOU READY?

Are you ready to make all your dreams come true? Can you imagine living the life you've always dreamed of living? What would make you ecstatically happy, fulfilled, and elated to be alive?

Allow me to share a story with you. My close friend is living all of his dreams. He's done everything he's ever dreamed of doing and more—and so can you. My pal calls his activities, adventures. He looks forward to and recommends that we all do the same or more.

Obviously we're talking about the dreams of your own choosing, because dreams don't have deadlines. I share this with you because you've never heard of my friend and his story is guaranteed to inspire you to think deeply, to think anew, and to feel refreshed and feel new possibilities when you realize others have actually lived their dreams.

This pal of mine explored the Amazon for three weeks with a native guide and loved every minute of the experience. He's flown a private plane, an ultralight. He's piloted a helicopter, a jet plane, and a space shuttle simulator. He's raced

Formula One Dodge cars. He directed the orchestra of my favorite play with music that lives in my mind forever and probably yours too—The Phantom of the Opera.

He's played the lead as Barnum in a major Broadway production—balancing while walking on a tightrope, singing. And he told me that when the play was over and they went to take the final curtain calls to a standing ovation, he was astounded as all the other actors stood back and let him go out there solo to receive the applause. It gives me goose bumps to recount that to you.

He played as a clown in the Barnum and Bailey Circus. He watched an open heart surgery up close and personal. He loves plays and goes to as many as two a week in New York City where he lives. He especially loves to go backstage and received special permission to watch *The Lion King* from behind the scenes and see how the whole technology and all the techies worked.

Currently, he's a professor at a medical school where he teaches pathology three hours a week because he loves to share and teach. He doesn't need to, but he loves to. As I share this with you, he's off on another exotic holiday in Belize where he's scuba diving at the world's second largest reef. He's piloted a submarine and dozens of more activities, which as I said, he calls adventures. And he showed me his list of what he has in store for the future.

SELLING THE BROOKLYN BRIDGE

Now the story I think you're going to like best is the one about how he sold the Brooklyn Bridge—as you know that's the oldest joke in the world. But seriously, my pal was watching a television show and workers were pulling up all the wooden planks from the 150-year-old Brooklyn Bridge. Fortuitously, the television videographer's lens captured the name of the truck hauling service and my friend noticed the 1-800 phone number. He instantly wrote down the number and immediately dialed the number. He actually watched a man hauling the planks answer his phone on TV. My buddy asked, "What are you doing with all those wooden planks?"

The guy said, "We're going to burn them. Why?"

My pal said, "For five hundred dollars, would you drive the planks over to my place in New Jersey?"

The answer, "Give me your address. Buddy, I didn't fall off the turnip truck."

My friend quickly wrote a publicity release and sold authenticated slivers of the Brooklyn Bridge, in little plastic vials, for $14.95 plus $2 shipping and handling.

Well, the media went wild: New Jersey Man Sells the Brooklyn Bridge! ABC, NBC, and CBS News interviewed him and the story went around the world. He thought it'd be short-lived, but it kept gaining ground and then the world press caught wind of it too. It's amazing the money that poured into his mailbox. And now he's a self-published author of eleven books. He sold every one of them only using publicity, media hype. He is his only outlet, and he won't write or do a book unless he knows he's going to receive a million dollars in his mailbox.

My friend Paul Hartunian has traveled everywhere and played full out. As a teacher in medical school, he loves his students—yet they have no idea who their teacher really is or what ecstatically exciting things he's doing or done, because he is quietly effective. And unless you knew him and were up close and personal with him, you'd never hear his story.

Why don't *you* be center stage in life? Just like my friend Paul was center stage in a Broadway play and at the end took all the bows—you can too because all of life is a stage. It's not just for Dr. Paul Hartunian. He's a humble gentleman with a magnificent mind and an enormous spirit. Why not decide that you're going to live the exquisite adventure of adventures and understand that your dreams don't have any deadlines.

A NEW DIRECTION AND DESTINATION

As I start this book sharing one man's story I think it's a story of every person—it's my story, it's your story, it's our story because no dream has a deadline unless *you* put a deadline on it. And if it doesn't get reached, why not expand it? Paul has done it in his own inimitable but duplicatable way. You and I can do the same, or more, if you want to. If you have the will and if you have two things: one is the desire, the idea; and then all it takes is one key commitment. Then, wow, your future takes on a new importance, a new direction.

One of my colleagues and friend Jim Rohn wisely and correctly said, "When you change your direction, you automatically change your destination." These ideas are to give you new hope and a promise for an ever more titillating future, one that hits you at the depth of your being so you emanate out from the core to the stuff that you're magnificently passionate about. You and you alone can change your direction, and therefore your destinations.

I want to help you make your life a masterpiece, an exciting story. We're sharing a story that makes a difference—one that's fun, glorious, joyous, and memorable. As you probably know, Bob Dylan said, "I'll let you be in my dreams, if you'll let me be in yours." Well, one of my dreams came true. I dreamed that someday I'd get to do some taping for the world's largest audio production company, Nightingale-Conant Corporation. I even had Vic Conant with me in my studio, which just wowed my soul.

AGE AND TIME

The great baseball player Satchel Paige pitched in the Major Leagues when he was at least 60 years old. No one, including himself, knew exactly when Satchel had been born. Somebody asked him, "How do you perform as a pro athlete while other people of this generation are making it easy in retirement?" Paige replied with a question of his own, and it's a question you might want to ask yourself. Paige asked, "How old would you be if you didn't know how old you are?"

For most of human history people did not keep track of time the way we do today. Even in ancient civilizations people did not think of themselves as 30, 40, or 50. People's ages were reckoned by the attitudes they displayed, by what they could do physically, emotionally, spiritually, and by their life and lifestyle.

I've been studying about the Aboriginals and what they do as they write their life map. When a kid hits about 13 years old, they do their "walkabout." They walk about where their ancestors walked about, and that's how they determine time. So time is different in different places—to an American it is one thing, to an Aboriginal it's another.

I'm going to ask you to expand some of your awareness of what time might be and even study some other looks at time as we go through this book.

In the old days, a young person was somebody who had exuberance but perhaps lacked wisdom. A mature person routined that youthful energy and willingness and vitality to take chances, but tempered it with knowledge and wise insight. An old person was somebody whose life had begun to contract not only physically and mentally and spiritually, but they narrowed their ranges of interest. It's sort of like what happens in myopia, nearsightedness; when people get macular degeneration their eyesight starts to narrow until it is so low that it's at 1 percent.

What I'm saying is, don't narrow your range; rather, open it up 360 degrees, representing the full spectrum of possibilities. I want you to have all the colors, all the richness, all the vitality, all the zest, all the joy, all the exquisite excitement, and all the interesting ideas instead of letting them contract, which is the mental model most people live—let's have them expand. Let's have you become richer, deeper.

Sometimes when people are interviewing for a position, they are told that they are over-qualified or over-trained. I don't think that's possible because no one was born under-endowed, we were born over-endowed. We've got 18 billion bountiful, beautiful, totally available brain cells waiting to come to work. The concept of an old person yesterday is no longer the concept that we have in this new millennium. You and I have a path before us that can be smooth, beautiful, and perfect. Old doesn't have to be old anymore.

We are starting to reverse the whole aging process—and we're heading into a world where the date on your birth certificate is going to be a lot less important than:

- What you know

- Who you are

- How you think

- What you value

- What is deeply important and meaningful to you

- How you want to impact society

- How you want to have your success go to significance

- Where you source and serve others in ways that maybe they never even thought they could be sourced and served.

So in those terms, what age do you see yourself at right now?

Close your outer eyes, assuming you're not driving, and open your inner eyes and see yourself in your imagination, as if you're ageless and timeless being asked how old you are. What is your response? My response would be that I'm about 28 years old. I'm actually over twice that but it's time to rethink this stuff of age and time.

In fact, let's throw out the clock. I've been in a lot of business meetings where the people in attendance are financially successful. And I've watched as a majordomo takes an alarm clock up on stage and then takes a sledgehammer and crashes it down, demolishing the clock. The whole audience erupts into raucous roaring applause.

Well, why not do that? Why not get rid of the alarm clock and start thinking in different terms. How much life force energy do I have? What am I enthused about? Enthusiasm means spirit within shown without. What am I rip-roaring tuned in about? What is it that I love? And where is it that I can exude and share my wisdom and my growth and my insight and my foresight? How is it that I can create the future of my heart's desire?

Scott Fitzgerald said there are no second acts in American lives. I think that was true when he wrote it, but that was a long time ago. He of course was a great writer with a lot of recognition; but I think today that we all get to have a third act and a fourth act because we're in a new time. Not only are there going to be second, third, fourth, fifth, sixth, seventh acts—but people are going to have their 40th year, 50, 60, 70; and there are more centurions, 100-year-olds, than ever before.

One time when I was presenting a talk, I noticed a man in the front row. People who sit in the front row are usually the hungriest, the ones who want to absorb the most—the ones who really want to get baptized almost by the saliva of speakers like me who try to be forceful and energetic and tuned in and turned on.

This guy was obviously a senior; and after being introduced to him, I learned that he was a podiatrist for more than fifty years of his life and was the long-term free-throw instructor with the Chicago Bulls, even wrote a book titled *Free Throw.* He was the world's free throw champion according to *The Guinness Book of World Records.* At 74 years old, he made 2,750 free throws in a row without a single miss. He spent his retirement sharing his free-throw secrets. I introduced Dr. Tom Amberry to the audience and he received a standing ovation.

When I met Dr. Tom, he was turning 80 years old and he thought that he was just beginning his life. There was a journalist there who wanted to interview me and I said to the journalist, "You should interview this guy—this guy is tomorrow. This guy's alive and excited and he wants to have everybody here learn how to do free throws!" Now basketball has never been my sport, but I believe because he believed that I could get into it.

One of the many things I'll be teaching throughout this book is that if you're going to be great, you have to have one major idea, one desire, and one key player. Then, voila! Your life is going to change and your fortune and your future is going to be better and richer.

I knew that if I really wanted to get into basketball, I'd get up close and tight with this guy. I'm saying that there's going to be that type of mentor for everybody, everywhere. And that's why there is never a deadline attached to a dream.

MENTORSHIP—THE BEGINNING

There will always be someone whose story can be very instructive about the possibilities that always lie in wait for us. The danger, though, is in thinking that if you can't hit a home run your first time at bat, you might as well take the baseball and go home.

I have to tell you my own story. Twenty-five years ago I was a wannabe speaker and I was out speaking around. I had a great little title on one of my talks: "How to Triple Your Income and Double Your Time Off." I was talking in San Diego as a breakout speaker and the guy sitting in the front row was Dr. Jack Canfield. He was an absorbent sponge drinking it all in. At the end of the talk he said, "Look, can we go to lunch?" We went to lunch together, befriended each other, and got together a lot. I attended all his seminars; he attended all mine. At the time, I was 44 years old and Jack was 48.

Then one time I went to Los Angeles to the polo club where he was talking to a breakfast group, the Inside Edge. He wowed my soul that morning; he was better than ever. We had breakfast together and I said, "Hey, Jack, what's cool, what's new, what's happening in your life?"

He said, "I'm going to write a book titled *Happy Little Stories.*" And he told me about the stories.

"I think we ought to do this book together and I really don't like that title very much. I don't think it has much strength," I told him. Nowadays we teach to never do a book unless you have a great title; that's the first and most important part. Then you have to have a great book and then great marketing, and great everything behind it to be a best seller.

But we started working on it anyway, without a title. I sent him some stories and we decided we would be 50/50 partners. We worked and worked and we thought we could do it in three months. Both of us had written a lot of books.

I'd written *Future Diary, The Miracle of Tithing,* and *How to Achieve Total Prosperity.* Jack had the all-time education best seller at that time, selling more than 400,000 copies, titled *101 Ways to Build Self-Esteem* in a classroom.

So we thought we knew how to write a book. But what we were really doing, though we couldn't see it while we were in the depths of working and sweating and stressing, was building a pattern for how to write a book series called *Chicken Soup for the Soul.* What was supposed to take three months actually took three years and became an act of love and labor and disagreement and discussion. Our spouses said, "Are you sure you guys aren't just goofing around because you are practically living together and we almost never see you."

SHOE LEATHER EXPRESS

Then we went to New York with a great agent. We did the "shoe leather express" and thirty-three major publishers all said, "Hit the road, Jack." I said, "Okay, if you don't like him, I'm a nice guy." We still got evicted. Then our agent wrote us a letter saying, "Look, I just don't think you're ever going to sell those sappy little stories." I told him, "We're not selling little stories. We're offering heart-touching, soul-penetrating stories—we're selling stories that will make people's hearts sing and give them renewed hope."

My immigrant parents taught me that America had hope written on it. I saw this as our big goal. Jack saw it as our big goal. Yet we were told that we should oscillate on it and go back and do what we knew how to do. But I said no, this is the thing that's going to change our lives.

Jack called one day and told me that the Book Expo was coming to Los Angeles. I'd been working all month and was dog tired and hadn't seen my wife and family much, but he said matter-of-factly, "On May 17th we're going to the Book Expo...we'll just go for two hours."

Well when I got in there, it was the place of places! I never thought I would be in a place like that. There was every book I could ever possibly want. Steven Spielberg was there, Margaret Thatcher was there, former presidents were there—for me, that was Heaven. So Jack and I were there laboring around with heavy backpacks filled with three-ring binders of *Chicken Soup.* We got turned down by 134 more people. Some took it and read it and discounted us. One small publisher, Health Communications, with two partners, said, "We'll take it home and read it overnight. You guys come back tomorrow morning."

Oh my gosh, I thought, *I have to come back tomorrow? On Sunday? I'm gonna have to miss church.* But it was so import-ant to me. There's a time in each and every person's life when you have to take your dream and pedestalize it and say, "Look, this is the most important thing." Temporarily, you have to sacrifice your family. You front-end it with your family say-ing, "Look, I'm going to make it up to you. Here's the tradeoff. Here's the compromise. I'll take you on a wonderful vaca-tion...." Do whatever you have to do.

But you also have to say something like, "This dream is what's consuming me. The dream is making my life valuable right now; the dream is what I came to realize; it's what I have to do; it's what I'm passionately on purpose about; it's what I came to do."

Jack and I were both what the world calls "middle age." I don't think people hit middle age until we're 70 or 80 and really start to get refined; but the point is, we needed to do this book now. The next day they called us and Gary Seidler, one of the two partners, said, "I cried all over my silk shirt. I think this will make it." And his partner, Peter Vegso, said, "If you guys can guarantee that you will buy twenty thousand books at six dollars each, we will do it." Well, we had already pre-sold that many, so we knew that it was going to be a hitter for us. So, we signed a contract and we were off and running.

We wanted to sell a million and a half in a year and a half. We asked all of our friends to pre-buy 100 copies. One friend, Raymond Aaron, bought 1,700 copies.

We worked our butts off. We read two books that really changed our lives. One was by Dr. Jeffrey Lant, *How to Make a Whole Lot More Than $1,000,000.* The other was by John Kremer, *1001 Ways to Market Your Books.* We read them. We underlined. We highlighted. The books triggered ideas for us. We posted 1,094 little yellow stickies in Jack's office in Culver City, covering the whole wall. Then we started prioritizing to get clear what we wanted to do and how we wanted to do it. We had the why and the how clear in our minds. We decided that we were going to do it! That first book sold 1,300,000 the first year. Then we were told that we were supposed to do one book every other year.

But we went from one book the first year to another book the second year. Then we started breaking all the book sales records and got into *The Guinness Book of World Records.* We tithed on every book that we did. Jack and I tithed each book's profits to a different charity, which really made our hearts sing. Whether it's the Red Cross or whatever, that's one of the little secrets of success. We've had a lot of people help us—because the stories have helped them. The number of people who came up to Jack and me at seminars or book signings was amazing.

CHAPTER 2

BURNING PASSION

We were doing books in a horizontal way—*Chicken Soup for the Soul* 1 through 6. So then we decided to market vertically and expanded to *Chicken Soup for the Women's Soul* and that market rocked. We followed that with *Chicken Soup for the Mother's Soul.* For two years in a row, that book was number one on all three lists—*Publishers Weekly, USA Today,* and *The New York Times.* We were the only ones to have ever done that.

It's amazing to us that we could come out of relative obscurity to become so successful. But it's possible when you have a burning desire and a passionate, continuing commitment. You can borrow awareness; you can borrow money; you can borrow distribution; you can borrow talent; you can borrow stories; you can borrow everything else you need and that's what we did. But we started and maintained our desire and commitment.

When Jack and I were on a book tour for *Chicken Soup for the Soul 2,* I remember that every morning we had to get up at 4 a.m. We were on major TV shows in different cities at six o'clock. Then we sat for various media all day long, did book signings, and at night we presented a seminar usually to about a thousand people. This time *Dateline* staff were traveling with us. We had done twenty-five days in a row and one morning Jack and I were up early again. I'm staggering around, totally sleep deprived, and said, "I'm not going to make it. I have to quit."

He said, "Surrender. All you have to do is hang in three more days and we're number one." Well, our second book became a number-one best seller, and our first book became number two, which no one had ever done in such a short time. So then we decided to do two books a year and then we went up to four books a year; and this year we're coming up with twelve new books. I'm thankful to say that it's still working for us—and we're blessed being blessed.

We did *Chicken Soup for the Veteran's Soul* because Jack and I both have the heartfelt belief that veterans haven't been acknowledged, haven't been thanked. The *Chicken Soup* possibilities today are infinite. All I want to do is our example with you and see you break through with your dreams. Right now may seem shaky. They may not feel like they're well-grounded, they may not feel firm, and they may not have a foundation. But if you take heed and listen to what I have to share, you too will be blessed. Dreams *don't* have deadlines—if you tell yourself that multiple times until it saturates, permeates, penetrates, and fills the inner spaces of your being until you take *ownership* of the concept, you will change your life. At the front end, you may want to reject some of the concepts I'm going to share with you, which is natural and normal. But if you are where you want to be, you wouldn't have the inspiration or discontent to want to read this book and move to your next level.

MOVE TO YOUR NEXT LEVEL

I want to help you go to your next level. Together we are going to do it with stories, facts, and statistics that involve your right brain and your left brain. You'll go to places you didn't even know you could go. Maybe you haven't given yourself permission. Maybe you've forgotten about it. Maybe you have hidden it in a resource cubbyhole of your mind. Dust it off; dust off the dreams you have forgotten about.

This *Dreams Don't Have Deadlines* idea has been so exquisitely exciting that it's prompted me to revitalize some of the dreams and the hopes and prayers that I've had in the past. One night after attending a Horatio Alger awards presentation, I couldn't sleep. I got up and wrote down ten principles that fit this idea. Maybe you need to write the same for yourself.

As matter of fact, I'm going to give you that as one your voluntary, mandatory homework assignments. See if it doesn't wake up some dreams in you. Then take that into your conversations at the dinner table with your family or friends. Talk about your dreams and ideas and it'll wake up possibilities that you can't even imagine. Now is the time to invest in yourself; invest your time, invest your mind, invest your spirit, invest your soul.

Throughout these pages, I want to talk to you heart to heart and soul to soul. I want you to have a comprehensive change that exalts you and takes you to the next level beyond where even you think you can go now. It's time for you to rewrite your story. It's time for me to rewrite mine.

DO MORE, BE MORE

You're going to read how every seven years you're going to do more and change what you do and how you do it. It's going to be one the most exalted, fun experiences ever, because you're going to make your work your play, and you're going to make your future a joyous heart center that attracts you with excitement from the fiber of your being. I never gave up on my dreams and I want you to never give up on yours.

Jack Canfield and I have sold in excess of 500 million copies worldwide of *Chicken Soup for the Soul*. We have more than 250 titles that have been translated into 43 languages and have been published in more than 100 countries. We hope to sell a billion copies. I can tell you that because for a lot of reasons I think it's going to happen. Part of the reason is that we're at the point in life where we have eliminated all the dross. We know what really matters—the few things that we have to do and concentrate on.

Jim Rohn said in every discipline and every area of your life there's only three, four, five, six, or maybe seven things that you have to focus on; and if you just keep paying attention to them and keep scanning the horizon—sort of the dashboard of the management of your life—you'll get them done. That's what Jack and I are doing because we know what it takes to get stuff done.

Different people reach their model at different ages, so let's get refreshed, revitalized, and rethink life. Because our physical bodies, our physiology, changes every seven years, let's change what we do and how we do it every seven years. Let's be people of transformation. My father grew up knowing that he was going to be a baker because that's the model he came from. But today dreams don't have deadlines. It's a time for a brand-new model.

I want to emphasize that when I use *Chicken Soup for the Soul* as our example, it wasn't an end, it was a beginning. It allowed me to reinvent myself from a speaker to a best-selling author. Jack and I pinch ourselves because we've been the world's best-selling nonfiction authors. We pursued it as a dream and set it as a high benchmark. We broke all the rules; that's why I think I have the authority and the credibility to talk about dreams not having deadlines. I want to help you to break through and see new realities and to get you to think in levels that you haven't thought before. I want to help you understand that life is a continuous process through which we get to grow and glow and show at levels that maybe no one's ever thought of before.

THEN WHAT?

Now I want to transition into a story that everyone knows. It's an archetypal story—one that is relevant to all cultures, all times, and all people. The story is Noah and the ark. Most people know the beginning of that story, that Noah was destined to save the world by building an ark and taking two of every kind of animal into the ark to save them from the flood. Then God placed a rainbow in the sky as a promise never to flood the earth again.

But what happened when Noah got out of the ark was a big mistake. There was the world all fresh and clean, a place of unlimited opportunity. Instead of setting forth confidently with a new plan to a new world, Noah sat down and got drunk. Now remember that people morph every seven years—what they do or how they do it. Why did Noah do that? My assumption is that Noah thought he was done—he could retire. I ran this thought by one of the great Bible scholars of our time, my friend Dr. John Maxwell. I also ran it by Dr. John Hagee. Both of them agreed that Noah thought he was finished, ready to retire.

I don't think people are supposed to retire. I think we're supposed to repurpose ourselves— because a boat that sits collects barnacles and an empty house attracts vermin. Don't go from something to nothing. Go from something to something better, something greater, something more wondrous.

Noah had a great success and that's what most people take away from the story. But he thought his work was done and I believe it wasn't. Your work is not done either. With my heart and soul and depth of the core of my being, I want you to repurpose yourself. I want you to not *retire* but to re-tire yourself. Put four new tires on your car self and take yourself wherever you want to go. I want you to turn on the engine and start your beingness to go where you want to go with it. One person can make a difference—and you're that one person.

Noah's retirement attitude caused him serious problems. I don't want retirement attitudes to cause you problems. I want you to reinterpret yourself and say, "Hey, I'm not going to quit no matter what my chronological age." What if you were to go inside your mind's eye, inside the stage of your imagination, to see yourself on a screen as the person you want to be. You see yourself as healthy and financially fit as you want to be, having all the social graces you want, traveling when you want as much as you want, hanging out up close and personal with the people you want to be with. You want to be accomplishing great things and sourcing and serving causes that maybe no one else is thinking about but you. The best is yet to be and you can be more successful than you've ever been.

YOUTH IS A PARADIGM

Remember that the United States is a young country. We celebrate youth; but youth is a spirit. Youth is an inside decision. Youth is a paradigm that you make. It is a decision.

My friend Art Linkletter was 97 years young when he passed away in 2010. Art was the one who brought the hula hoop to the United States and made a fortune. He was simultaneously on ABC, NBC, and CBS. At 89, he had in excess of 20,000 employees and is still doing superlatively well. In 2006, we wrote a book together, *How to Make the Rest of Your Life the Best of Your Life.* It's so exciting what you can do, no matter your age. Art told my wife and I when we had lunch with him in Hollywood one day, "You know, I don't feel old at eighty-nine. I'm really good for a hundred and fifty." Art rejuvenated himself top down, inside out. His spirit was young.

One of the ways you stay young is to hang out with young people. And I want you to rejuvenate the benefits of your good life with good thinking, good spiritual practice, good nutrition, and good exercise—because when we do right thinking, right action, we're going to get the right results. That statement is documented and proven—there's just no question about it. There is no good reason you should limit yourself by a clock or a calendar that seems to tell you life should be X.

PAST, PRESENT, FUTURE

I am encouraging you to think in terms of getting bigger and better rather than smaller and contractive—why not be expansive? There are three kinds of people: a past person who says, "Back when I was in high school I was a football star," "I was the head cheerleader," or whatever. There is a present person who can see only what's happening in the here and now. And then there's the future-oriented person who can see the past in a deeper way. The better you know the past the better you can integrate it and take it into the future in a rich and fully dynamic way to more purposefully live now and take it forward.

So I'm going to ask you to focus on the future rather than the past. Think about being able to cover more territory to reach more people, serve greater, go faster and further than ever before. You can do that regardless of when you were born with the amazing technologies that have come into being in the past twenty years. Technology allows us to do the impossible. Before the telephone it was impossible to *communicate* around the world. Before Orville and Wilbur Wright we couldn't *travel* around the world.

We're in extraordinary times and technology leverages us. But instead of letting technology scare you, why not embrace it, believing that it's going to source and serve you to do what you couldn't do before. What was impossible yesterday is possible today.

The current view of aging is going to change by the time you're finished with this book. I'm confident you're going to agree with me about that. Why not decide that you're going to create not only a personal future, but a personal history based on exquisite excitement and dreams that don't have deadlines? For proof that this goal can be accomplished, all I have to do is look over the events of my own life. And all I'm doing is sharing my example with you.

Your Life Inventory

So now I'm going to take you through a brief inventory not just of your goals but of your dreams, when you were in your teens or even before. What were the things you wanted to do or to accomplish or the things that you wanted to invent or the ideas you wanted to explore? Most importantly, who is the person you wanted to be? Write all this down. My cliché is: Don't think it, ink it. Delegate it to document in whatever form seems comfortable to you.

Or you might be more comfortable typing on a computer like I am. Or maybe you write in a journal. Jim Rohn said when you transition out of life, the thing you want to give your kids more than wealth is your journals. Wouldn't it be nice for you to get to read the journals of your parents and your grandparents and great-grandparents?

I want you to get comfortable with writing. I've been on Oprah Winfrey's show three times and she said that when she was making the movie *Color Purple* with Steven Spielberg, she was sitting with him at lunch one day and he was drawing and writing in his journal. When she asked him what he was doing, he said, "I'm drawing Dreamworks." I don't know what your position is on Spielberg, but my position is that he's a Walt Disney of our time; the greatest media contributor. Yet when I read stories about him, he says, "All I am is a story-teller," and I think, *Well, that's all I am.*

Oprah leaned over to Spielberg and said, "Do you mind if I copy that down?" She copied it and wrote her own business plan. And as you probably know, she was the first female African-American billionaire all because she journaled. And if you journal, do it in color. If you're writing spiritual stuff, use the color purple because that's the top of the rainbow. If you're doing heart stuff, write in pink; if moneymaking writing, use green. You pick the colors and then morph it. Make a list of things in several paragraphs, *create a future inventory of what you want to do*—not that you can afford to do, not that you have the talent to do, not that you have the people to do. Don't be judgmental. Most of us way underjudge ourselves. The word "sin" in the Bible is an Aramaic term that means to miss the mark, to miss the target; and the only way to miss the target is to not have a target. That's why *dreams don't have deadlines.*

YOUR 101 DREAMS

I'm going to ask you to write 101 dreams before you finish reading this book. I have more than 6,600 of them. All I'm asking you to do is take a chance. You have everything to gain and nothing to lose. When you write down your dreams, you're going to talk about them and keep adding to them. I want you to be totally imaginative. Just in case you think you need it,

I'm giving you permission to take away all the limitations, all the cobwebs, all the self-sabotaging behavior. You have the imprimatur of imprimaturs, the platinum American Express card—and metaphorically the camels will come up and bring you frankincense, myrrh, and all the gold you can handle.

The question is, how much do you want? What are you willing to go for to be outside the normal program and go find out that there's no limitation on imagination? *Imagination is the future of all reality.* In your imagination you are going to absorb what you are reading that will catalyze you, taking you to where you want to go—into that high-flying butterfly world—that's the self-fulfilling prophecy that we're focusing on.

It's not according to a clock or calendar—it's according to your imagination. Your imagination and your thinking makes it so.

YOUR LIFE TIMELINE

By now, I hope you have revisited your personal aspirations and have written your 101 dreams. I'm going to ask you to create one more written document—a timeline of your life focusing not on what you wanted to happen or what you dreamed would happen, but what actually took place over the years of your life. This timeline is sort of like that Aboriginal map from Australia that I mentioned earlier. Get some crayons and a poster board and draw a picture. This is something you want to keep. This is a document that you want to write on and see your life trajectory, your life story.

When I've been in seminars with one of the wisest women on the planet, Dr. Jean Houston, we show our timelines to each other and it expands us as we look back. It will be the same for you because when you see it, you'll say, "Oh, I forgot about that incident!" As you will read later in more detail, all you have when you look back on life are little snapshots, photographic memories of your life.

Now put these two documents side by side—your dream inventory of where you hope to go and your timeline of where you've been. What did you want to happen? Remember, this can be private. As you look at these two documents, how much difference do you see between them, and to what extent did you bring your deepest aspirations into the world?

I believe that *everyone* is coded at birth at a DNA and RNA level for greatness—not just one or two people or the heroes and heroines of our planet. I also think that at some young age we are told what we're going to do. When I was 16 years old, I was driving down Glen Flora Avenue in Waukegan, Illinois, where I was born. In one moment it was like time stopped and I went into that proverbial time warp. I saw myself in front of 80,000 people. I wondered what that meant. At that point, the only picture I had was of Elvis Presley who had that kind of audience or Billy Graham. And I thought, *I can't sing and I'm not a preacher...I'm only a kid. So what can I do?* Well, currently I present 50-75 seminars each year to many thousands of attendees. And I haven't had my biggest act yet. I think it's in front of me; and I think there's an act in my future that has a million audience members, and I know where that's going to be.

So, I'm asking you to brush off that dusty long-ago memory, remember it, revitalize it, and reinvigorate it because as you look at these two documents, you may think they don't have much in common. But I can promise you that when you do this same exercise next year and in five years and nine or ten years from now, you're going to see there's a lot more similarity between what you *hope* to do and what you've actually *done.*

The more things you hope for, the more things you'll do. I say it's not that you want too much, it's that you want too little. Most people don't put this great capacity to work. We are born over-endowed with 18 billion brain cells, but they can't get to work until we make the decision to let the subconscious make the provision.

When you put these ideas into action, your life's going to change. Your life is going to get infinitely better and that's what we're going to discuss in the following chapters. We'll look at some of the real-world, practical opportunities for people 40 and over. If you're younger, good for you! You will be ahead of those who aren't aware of how dreams don't have deadlines. No matter your chronological age, this is going to be an exciting and illuminating journey together.

SNAPSHOTS

As we end this chapter, let me revisit the point made at the outset. Many have been conditioned to believe that success happens early, if it's going to happen at all. I hope you're already beginning to see that isn't true. It often takes time to see the truth of any event, situation, and circumstance. Passage of time, the twists and turns that erode, even the real adversity we face is essential to our ultimate fulfillment. So choose to see the past as a prologue and the future as yet to be. Realize how what happened can enhance what's happening now and that it's part of the depth of your beingness and will impact your whole future.

The fact is, after a certain age our lives are remembered by a series, as you read earlier, of snapshots, mental pictures of where you've been, what you've done, and with whom. These are our mental moments of memory. Snapshots can have a positive or negative predisposition. So we need to create snapshots of memory that are worthy of our highest dreams and our loftiest aspirations and goals.

You need to develop positive, proactive pictures that attract you and draw you and bring you in. We want you to develop these proactive pictures; the best pictures that show you are thriving. And the more you do that, the better your future is going to turn out.

It's a great privilege to be a free person in a free society. But the most important thing is that you get to have a free mind and a free imagination—and you get to choose to remember and exalt the best of all freedoms, which is the freedom to pick the snapshots that you want to live in and thrive in, so you can be the best you can be and serve the world the best that it's ever been served as only you can do. Only you can choose to be free inside your mind no matter what your situation and circumstances. Your freedom of imagination gives you a greater, grander, and more terrific realization of life.

So let's get started on our journey now.

CHAPTER 3

THE CHALLENGE OF CHALLENGES

Businessman and millionaire Malcolm Forbes made the interesting observation about how our lives need to change as we get older. He said that if you think you're going at the same speed as you've always been going, you're actually slowing down because the world is generally speeding up—so you better get moving.

Forbes didn't really come online personally or professionally until he was more than 50 years young when he took over his late father's magazine, *Forbes* magazine. He discovered publicity was free and he had an outrageously entertaining idea that he would employ publicity as it had never been employed before. He became a motorcyclist who toured the world with friends on the back of his bike—friends like actress Elizabeth Taylor and Dr. Henry Kissinger. He created fantasy hot air balloons that looked like the country he was visiting. In Egypt his balloon looked like the Sphinx; in China like the Great Wall; in England like a British castle. It worked! His crazy life and lifestyle became front-page news and his magazine circulation and ad revenue went through the roof.

He bought eight outrageous castles. He had a $2 million bash in Tunisia at his castle and invited the world's who's who with all the requisite paparazzi. While there, he showed his Faberge egg collection and his toy soldier collection. They brought in his Highlander yacht, named the *Capitalist Tool,* on which he entertained royalty, presidents, leaders, and prospective clients. The Highlander was equipped with helicopters, jet skis, and all the amenities. I saw it for the first time when I was in Detroit, Michigan. He had a movie theater on it that would hold 500 people.

I wanted to see it for myself, but of course, there were bodyguards guarding it. But I went up close to one of them and asked, "Who's on the Highlander right now?"

"Onboard right now is the head of Chrysler, the head of Ford Motor Company, the head of GM, and the mayor of Detroit," he said. "Almost 100 percent buy from us after they've gone on our little tour and seen the cups with the different presidents who have toured the ship of all ships."

I thought, *someday I want a ship like that.*

Malcolm Forbes realized success late in life, but he fully enjoyed all of his successes. Now you may not be in a position to inherit a magazine, but as time passes you'll have new opportunities and even responsibilities to bring out the best in yourself, to reinvent yourself, to express what's best in you for your own sake and for the sake of the world around you and total humanity.

It's not just for Malcolm Forbes or Madonna or Oprah or Michael Jordan to reinvent themselves—it's for you. It's for me. It's for us. It's never too late. In this chapter you're going to see why you have both the opportunity and responsibility to realize your dreams. You will be introduced to information on practical tools to help you do that.

First, some facts and figures show why it's so important for older Americans to be productive, to add value, and to remain contributing members of society. We're going to look at why dreams must not have a deadline from a societal perspective.

My teacher, Bucky Fuller (R. Buckminster Fuller), said to my wife one night at dinner, "Patty, you don't own you. The universe owns you, and you're obligated to the universe to do all that you can do." That's why we're going to focus specifically on what our dreams are as an individual human being. We'll look at what our dreams were at earlier points in our life and whether they've changed or maybe even faded into the background.

SYNERGY

Then we'll see how you can reignite your dreams. You can get in touch with them again if you've lost touch. I want to light that candle of your life. If my candle's lit and yours isn't, we light your candle from my candle—and now the world is twice as bright. The synergy of it is that its fourfold as bright.

Let's say there are a thousand people in the room called our life. I light your candle, you light somebody else's, and soon we have the whole place megawatted and illuminated. That is what *Dreams Don't Have Deadlines* is all about—being illuminated individually and then illuminated collectively. And that's why we're looking at reigniting dreams that you may have lost touch with. When you are reignited, you're on fire. As you're on fire, it translates into the people around you, and they'll start getting on fire. Wouldn't it be nice if everybody was on fire?

The conversations that are the most exciting are when people are talking about what makes them wired, that tunes them in and turns them on. Let's be those people. Let's get started with some facts about our country today.

STATS

Those belonging to the baby boomer generation, of which I'm one, were born from 1944 to 1964. There are about 78 million of us in the United States. The oldest of the baby boomers reached the age of 50 in 1996 and about 10,000 baby boomers are turning 65 every day. But that's just demographic data. The following are a few statistics that have very clear implications about how all Americans of whatever age are going to be living their lives in the years to come.

Allow me a preface statement about the Social Security system, or the insecurity system as some call it. I don't want you to depend on something that's not secure. It was modeled after Kaiser Wilhelm's system in Germany and set up in 1935 by then-president Franklin D. Roosevelt. Unfortunately, there wasn't any program set in place that looked realistically into the future. Demographically people died at 45, so there was no worry about paying off people at 65.

But then people starting setting a goal of retiring at 65 and drawing out the money they put into the Social Security system. So now let me do the hard statistics. In the middle years of the 20th century, there were about 16 workers for every retired American. In other words, there were 16 people pay-ing into Social Security for every person drawing money out of it. There's 60 people around to do the work of our society for every person who is no longer working.

But at the start of the 21st century, there are only three workers for every retired person. And in 30 years, there will be only two such workers. As you can see, that is not going to pay. I think you can start to see some of the concerns that num-bers like that raise, not just for the Social Security system but also for accomplishing the everyday work of our country. And that's only the start. Let's look at a few more facts and figures.

In 1965, almost 60 percent of Americans past the age of 55 were still in the workforce. Today that figure is less than 40 percent and it's 40 percent of a much larger population. About 70 percent of all Social Security recipients are receiving bene-fits before the age of 65.

Full retirement age had been 65 for many years. However, beginning with people born in 1938 or later, that age gradu-ally increases until it reaches 67 for people born after 1959. The 1983 Social Security Amendments included a provision for raising the full retirement age beginning with people born in 1938 or later. Congress cited improvements in the health of older people and increases in average life expectancy as pri-mary reasons for increasing the normal retirement age. Today, if you start receiving retirement benefits at age 62, you will get 80 percent of the monthly benefit.

Although this change has helped, it is still doubtful that the Social Security system can continue to function indef-initely. Not to mention our health care system, including

Medicare. I discuss how to become debt-free, stress-free, and set free in a later chapter.

I want you to consider what the world's most famous gerontologist, my friend Dr. Ken Dychtwald has to say. Ken recommends that you have a goal of creating at least $2 million net worth when you retire to be debt-free. Why? Because you live longer in retirement than you do working. We're going to spend more on elder care than we ever spent on childcare. The bottom line—you need to be self-responsible, self-sufficient, and self-financed to be truly free. Write that down as part of your goals that we talked about in the last chapter.

Something unprecedented is taking place in the United States. There's an enormous demographic change; the aging population is on a scale that's never ever happened before. We've never had a population like we've got before. Up to 100 years ago, there were only one billion people worldwide. But in the last hundred years, the world population is up to 7.7 billion people. The population of the United States in 1920 was 106 million and in 2020 it is 330 million.

Our society is still looking at the post-50 group as if it were comprised of the same number of people as in the past, which is a big mistake. The numbers are growing and so are their needs. Ancient spiritual law says, "Be fruitful, multiply, replenish." It never said quit being fruitful at age 59, 65, or 72, just because you may be financially secure.

Rather, if you have money, I encourage you to *go from success to significance.* That's where you serve others greatly and serve for the sake of serving, care for the sake of caring, love for the sake of loving. What's more, many older Americans are still behaving the way that older people did in the past, despite the fact that this is counter to their best interests as well as the best interests of the country. As mentioned earlier about the boat and the empty house deteriorating, if you don't use your body it atrophies. Rather than atrophying, I want you to build yourself up, get stronger, get more dynamic, and get more purposeful.

For example, people are retiring earlier because there are financial incentives for them to do so. Many of the nation's largest employers urge older workers to leave early through the structure of the benefit plans; and sure enough, the people retire early because it seems to make good financial sense.

All I'm saying is *transition from something to something better.* Why not consider being a free agent and doing something brand-new. Be an entrepreneur; create something great as we're looking at the problem here on a go-forward basis. You may think that the government's going to take care of it. That's the opposite of what I'm saying. I'm saying consider the entrepreneurial route, the free-enterprise route where you create some free-enterprise activity that makes your heart sing. Consider something that is brand-new and sources and serves people—and you get paid for it. Possibly a charitable philanthropy can be part of it as well.

There are a lot of financial interests at work in the retirement issue besides just the company pension plan. I'm asking you to pay attention to some of the ads that are running on TV, in magazines, and on credible websites. See what mutual funds and banks and retirement communities are doing as an effort to get a big piece of the financial pie that the baby boomer generation represents. But most of the time they're going about it the wrong way. Often they're showing golf courses and secluded beaches and they're suggesting that you may not have enough money to afford the gold golf course or that secluded beach. So you better put your money into their retirement fund now.

But there's really a more interesting part. The truth is, a majority of this generation doesn't want that kind of future. They don't identify with the golden years concept that may appeal to previous generations who lived through world wars and economic depressions. This generation wants continued challenges, continued opportunities, and a society that lets them fulfill their desires.

THE CHALLENGE OF CHALLENGES

I want to talk to you about the challenge of challenges. Dr. Robert Muller (1923-2010), former Assistant Secretary-General of the United Nations, was a great speaker, great thinker, and great writer who tried to sign every one of his books so that everyone who bought it would feel a personal connection with him, which I admired.

One of his books that is now out of print was titled, *The Encyclopedia of World Problems and Human Potential*. It contained all the world's problems and all of the world's not-yet-implemented solutions. The bad news, there were more than a thousand major problems. The good news is that the solutions outnumber the problems. And better news, as far as I'm concerned, is that *you* can come up with solutions. You're here to use your imagination and to come up with solutions that have never been thought of before. And when you start having little mastermind groups and dream team groups, you can come up with solutions that no one's ever cogitated, ruminated, and meditated about.

We're just going to talk briefly here about this mastermind group or what I call a dream team or what I call pairing and sharing. We talk about this in-depth later. Each person is providentially incomplete. If you hold up your two index fingers and place them together, it isn't two but it's the power of eleven. Everyone achieves more together is the old cliché, but the new rewrite that I've done is *together everyone achieves miracles* because it's only when you have a team that you create miracles.

One of my new team members is a Nightingale-Conant artist named Bob Allen who's done multiple streams of income and is a superstar in his own right. He and I are doing breakthrough after breakthrough; we're doing stuff that everyone said can't be done. But it *can* be done when you put together the right team of people who think right, talk right, act right, make the right decisions and are committed to getting the right results for everyone. This collaboration goes to a higher level because you start dealing with an infinite system, and I don't think an individual alone can do that.

Nobody was ever a lone Lone Ranger. They called him the Lone Ranger, but he had Tonto, his friend. A flashlight only works if has two batteries. I want you to be an illumined person with an illumined soul—someone who is so radiant that you become a beacon on a hill for others. It's possible if you decide to become the bigger you. Your sphere will interface with other spheres of energy that you don't know yet; and voila! the world will work for 100 percent of humanity.

I know you may be thinking that's pretty idealistic to have Heaven on earth. But it's a concept that we can truly embrace and will serve to reignite our passion, our vigor, our interest. And now you may be thinking, *Hey, can I really do that?*

A CRISIS OF CONSCIOUSNESS

Twenty-eight years ago I was bankrupt and upside down; I fell out of the sky and crashed and burned and literally wanted to commit suicide for a while because I thought my net worth and my self-worth were the same. Then I wondered, *Someday could I have a home where there are fresh flowers on all the tables every day? Someday could I grow all my own fresh, organic live fruits and vegetables?* That someday is now for me.

As I have it for me, I want to expand it for thee; and I want to expand it for everyone because there's more than enough. The only crisis on the planet is a crisis of consciousness. There's no lack of money. Just in America we have a circulation of gross national product of $28 trillion. And that means that there's millions of dollars of wealth available to you. But wealth is top down, inside out created, which is discussed in the next chapter. There are more than enough resources; there are more than enough possibilities; and there are more than enough needs for us to flat-out do what we can with what we have to make life better for everybody else.

Look for the people in your life who can help you build your dream team. They are up close and personal but maybe you haven't seen them as they can be. When you're part of a dream team, you see more in them than they see in them-selves. The first three years Michael Jordan was playing basketball he sat on the bench, because he was told he wasn't good enough. So as a high school student, what did he do? He started shooting a thousand jumpshots a day. He did the dis-cipline; you have to do your discipline. I don't know what your discipline is, but you have to figure it out and then discipline yourself. It's like the maestro who was asked by a tourist in New York City, "How do you get to Carnegie Hall?" And the old maestro said, "Practice, practice, practice." Michael Jordan practiced, and his dreams came true.

BLOOM WHERE YOU ARE PLANTED

Begin where you are. Start where you're planted. Begin at once. Find one other person and work together until you get bigger and stronger and healthier and more whole—and you'll start to feel the vim, vigor, and vitality inside out.

I remember when I started my first mastermind gathering in Long Island, New York. Chip Collins and I met every week and not long after, the director of our small Chase Manhattan Bank started to attend, and then a minister with a church of five thousand. We met on Thursday mornings at 7:30 in a lit-tle deli on Long Island. Soon all of us were rip-roaring and doing better in our lives. The point is, everyone needs to start and bloom where they are planted.

You have the seed thought or you wouldn't have invested time in reading this book. You have the desire; you have the inspirational discontent. I can't know what it is, but if I were with you, I'd say, "Tell me what it is you want and why it is you want it in your heart of hearts. And if you'll do the doing, you'll have the having. But you have to understand—you have to be it, to do it, to have it."

Even when I was upside down financially, I was still being the speaker that I am today. I was being the best-selling author I am today. I was being the husband and father that I am today. I was being a contributor to the church system that means so much to me today.

For our book series, *The One Minute Millionaire,* we brought the forty best marketing minds together and we asked, "If your kid's life depended on it, what would you do to pre-sell a million books?" All forty people came up to the microphone and gave their answers, which we videotaped and audiotaped, and then transcribed to put into a workbook.

From that, we talked about putting together a TV show called *Solution,* where we examine a problem, like, "Let's clean the oceans so we don't lose 34 percent of the earth's seas." I was in negotiations with PBS about this idea. It was one of my dreams, because with more than seven billion people around the world, we have some major problems that need to be worked on.

I think you and I are here to solve those problems and this book has to do with getting inside your mind—to get you to start thinking. Maybe this will excite you, titillate you. Maybe it'll catalyze you, or maybe it'll irk you. But if it gets you to start thinking in some brand-new ways, we can come up with solutions. Just pick one, any one, and get into it, get behind it, and courageously volunteer to accomplish what all the king's horses and all the king's men couldn't do.

My wife and I founded Metamorphosis Energy, a clean energy company providing renewable energy solutions for any aspect of energy consumption. We believe that clean, green, sustainable energy will save the economy and the environment and paves the way for our children's future.

I say we're all living on one little spaceship called Earth, and it's fragile. I think it is your and my destiny to do something great that affects many people. I want to inspire you in-depth to do that. Because 80 percent of baby boomers say they want to continue working in some capacity after they've reached retirement age, I'm challenging you to pick the area that has confronted you, whatever it is, and tackle it.

I have a great friend, Collette, who has five children. Two of her kids were born with cystic fibrosis. She was a secretary, not making very much money, working for my dear friend Bob Allen. All a sudden she got involved in a network marketing company and decided she was going to make a fortune, as she had to pay to replace two lungs in her daughters who had cystic fibrosis. Now that she has gone from nowhere to somewhere great and learned how to have financial savvy, her daughters say, "I'm so proud to say she's my mom."

The other day I was interviewing Collette and she said, "I asked the doctors what it would cost to really solve this vicious, ugly, painful problem." They said, "One hundred million dollars." She told me, "During my lifetime I'm committed to putting it together and raising that kind of money."

You wonder why anyone would do that kind of volunteer work. I've won the Horatio Alger Award. Since 1947, about seven hundred individuals from all walks of life and diverse professional backgrounds have received the award. Many have come from rags to riches and we've been philanthropically charitable, trying to help at-risk kids. One of my peers is Dr. Peter Jeanette who worked on a cure for Christopher Reeve. Christopher Reeve was a movie star best known as Superman on the big screen and had a horse-riding accident that caused him to became a quadriplegic.

When in the hospital and faced with his future of never being able to walk or move or act again, he asked Dana, his wife, to call for the doctor.

"What is it?" asked the doctor.

Chris Reeve says, "What would it take to regenerate the spine?"

"We've been working on this a lot. As you know the electric eel, when cut, regenerates overnight. We have to raise fifty million dollars for the foundation so we can do this seminal research that will change the world."

Chris asked Dana to call his roommate from Juilliard, Robin Williams. Robin Williams comes to his friend and asked what he can do to help. Reeve tells him, "If I get fifty million dollars, we'll be able to regenerate my spine. And I hope we're good enough friends that I can appeal to you to be a source and serve me." Within two weeks later, Williams had a TV special that brought out the heart of America and raised the fifty million dollars, virtually overnight. That's worthwhile. That's important. Christopher Reeve passed away nine years after the accident, but the Christopher and Dana Reeve Foundation is still working and dedicated to curing spinal cord injury by funding innovative research and improving the quality of life for people living with paralysis.

BELIEVE YOU CAN DO IT

We have a fragile world and we all have to use our best mind- and brainpower to explore, look at it differently, be challenged by it, get into a deeply and say, "I'm here to make a difference." That's the issue I'm looking at with you. That's the kind of challenge I want you to take on. I'm saying that you probably have the talent, the resources, the network, and ability. Because you are reading this book, you've probably have some means that you've never thought of using. I'm urging you to pick a problem. Determine what is it that you want to do to, then work and keep working.

Maybe it seems impossible, but any dream may seem a little bit irrational at the front-end, but long term it's worth it. What if you write down that big goal we talked about in the previous chapter that seemed impossible? What if you break it down into doable daily bits and you start going for it with excitement? Your life will take on new energy; you start getting new friends; you have new vitality; you get new mentors.

It's pure and simple—America can't afford to allow 75 million people to vegetate, go fishing, play golf. That's not the right use of this great technology and talent called a human mind-body complex. It's so easy to say, "I can't do anything about it. I'm not enough. I don't know anyone. I don't have any wealth." Let's take the different point of view—believe you *can* do it. You *are* enough, you have enough. And if it's your issue, it's your time. You don't have to believe you can do it, just know that I believe you can do it—and then do it.

And let me say in advance, "Congratulations!" I may be congratulating you on something that will take your entire lifetime to complete. But I believe you can do it! It might be like Walt Disney who set a 100-year goal and my teacher Bucky Fuller who set a 100-year goal. On Disney's final day, on his death bed, an interviewer came in and said, "Epcot is being built by your friend Ken Ker and you're never going to see it."

Disney replied, "Don't you get it? If I didn't see it, you'd never see it."

Our friend Wally Amos, famous for the chocolate chip cookies told Jack and I the story about the little boy on the beach who tosses a starfish back into the sea. We put the now well-known story in one of our books. A crotchety old man couldn't see that the boy's effort was making a difference and says, "Boy, you're wasting your time." The youngster looks at the old man and says, "It made all the difference to that one."

MAKE A DIFFERENCE

I believe that what you do is going to make all the difference to you, and your friends, and to humanity into the future. If you take a challenge that is worthy of you. Pick a big challenge, pick something that excites you, pick something that's going make a difference to *that* one.

I don't know what it is you're supposed to do. As mentioned previously, create two lifelines: describe what already took place and describe what you want to do in the future. I'm challenging you to come *anew* with this thinking. Pretend you're 12 years old, back when there are no resistances, when you know you're not writing in marble. What is it that you want to do?

I want you to create a new life.

Maybe you want to do something professional like my friend who was the world's top free thrower of all times. Or my friend Art Linkletter who surfed six weeks during the summer and skied six weeks during the winter when he was 89 years young.

You're not here to give up, you're here to get into it and realize some of your earlier life fantasies. I don't know what you wanted to be good at. I don't know what challenges you physically, mentally, spiritually, financially, socially, or any way, but you can do more than you've ever done.

Yes, I want you to have a vacation and free days; but when you come back rejuvenated from that day on the beach or walking in nature, you're going to feel younger. You're going to ask yourself, *What are my dreams that don't have any deadlines. Where is that eclectic wisdom that I have inside? How can look deeper at what a really want? How can I pull out what I suppressed years ago and express it now? I'm ready to reignite it!*

Start now and make it the truth of who you can become. Let's reignite our dreams to the best of the best, the highest of the high. Let's think what hasn't been thought before—the breakthroughs only you can make.

I'm challenging you with all that's in me to be the catalyst that turns you on to the wealth of the challenge, the excitement of the dream. Remember, dreams don't have deadlines.

CHAPTER 4

GAINING AND GROWING WEALTH

One of my favorite topics is wealth—how to gain it, keep it, perpetuate it, and how to make it grow exponentially. There are ways to do all that after age 40 or 50 that are slightly different from what you might do in your 20s or 30s.

What does the word "wealth" mean to you? First and foremost it probably means money or a great abundance of valuable possessions, riches. That isn't the whole story, but it's a valid definition. You are going to be presented some solid information about how to create and keep financial wealth at any age. You can take the long route or the short route. I want to share with you how to create it and keep creating it so that it is ultimately self-perpetuating and self-generating. I want you to have a massive, passive, permanent, and ever-growing cash flow.

I want you to earn it, save it, invest it, multiply it, and then be charitable and philanthropic and give it away. Earlier I mentioned that Ken Dychtwald said you should have a minimum of $2 million when you're ready to retire. If that's not the truth of you yet, write down, "I'm so happy I'm an enlightened millionaire with in excess of two million dollars to retire on."

Then sign it. If you do that quick little exercise, it'll *impress* your subconscious so you *express* it on a screen of your future space. Do it now.

I want you to become an enlightened millionaire—it's a benchmark. An "enlightened millionaire" is somebody who comes from abundance and creates massive value for other people; somebody who is charitable and philanthropic and is going to make a significant difference.

So let's talk about why creating wealth is so important. Money makes life convenient. Jim Rohn said money makes you more of who you are. So if you're bad, you're going to be super-bad and if you're good, you can be super-good. Doing business and creating wealth is good for the soul. It's on trend with where humanity is right now. A motivational teacher of mine is Cavett Robert. He taught me that service is the rent we pay for the space we occupy. Christ said the greatest among you is a servant of all. Therefore the more social service you render, the happier and more fulfilled you will be.

Sometimes we meet young people who are just starting out in their careers. I've heard them say, "I want to make a million dollars before I'm forty." Or two million by the time they're 30 or maybe even before 25. In the early days of the dot coms, that was possible, but most of those didn't really have social value and real service value, so they became dot bombs. Of course without saying, there's anything wrong with that kind of youthful ambition, but let's just think for a minute what's behind that ambition.

Partly there there's a kind of fear behind it. It's the idea that if a big success doesn't come at an early point and fast, then you've wasted a lot of time. You have only one lifetime and you only have so many hours to make a living. You'd rather have a big mansion than a small house. You want to drive a nice car fifty years rather than only twenty or ten years. If you don't make that kind of wealth as soon as possible, you may think that you've wasted your time and maybe you've wasted your life. That's a young person's perspective; and to be honest about it, what other perspective could a young person have. But from my perspective, which has a bit of seasoning, why not think about what's important to create wealth as quickly as possible, as soundly as possible, and as safely as possible without violating our self, our culture, or our ecology. I think there are three reasons why it is important.

THREE IMPORTANT REASONS TO CREATE WEALTH

First, you need to create wealth so you don't have to worry about money all the time. The only people who worry more about money than the rich, are the poor. They think full time about it. You won't have to expend your energy on figuring out how you can pay your bills or how you can meet the other necessities of life. Those kinds of worries can be relegated to another place and time so you don't suffer the frustration the anger and resentment. Worry can make it a lot harder to focus on more interesting, more important, and more vital things of life.

The second reason why wealth is so important is so you can have the largest possible financial resources available to fulfill your biggest dreams, your most spectacular goals, your heart's desire—and you can fulfill those amazing aspirations.

The third and most important reason is something I shared with you earlier—we can live longer in retirement than we do working. With all the breakthroughs in health and medicine and science and gerontology, most of us are going to have a real shot at living to be 120 vital, healthy, happy, productive years. So what is it that you really want to do? If you can live longer and you're going to be more fulfilled, you better have that long list of cool stuff that you want to do.

As you read about wealth in this chapter, you will see two points of view. We look at the nuts and bolts and think in terms of prudence, safety, honesty, integrity, ethics, morality—and we'll think considerably bigger about ideas, visions, dreams, and hopes. We will look at how wealth can be used not just to meet the necessities, but to realize all of our soul's desires. That's the fun part! To get to be in control of the basics, stand on top of them, and then money allows you to control your life rather than let money control you. Please understand that I want *you* to be the master of money, not for money to master you.

FOUR AREAS OF WEALTH BUILDING

So let's look We will look at how at four very fundamental areas of wealth building for people in their 40s, 50s, and beyond. How much money do you need? Two million dollars by retirement is suggested, and then you can write that backward to wherever you are right now.

First you need wealth to meet the necessities. Then you need wealth to do those things in your timeline—the things you not only *have* to do, but more importantly the things you *want* to do, the things you've always dreamed of doing, the things you would do if you had more than enough to do them. I'd like you to think through those things.

Next, evaluate your cash flow. Once you have a clear idea of the amount of money you need, think about where it's coming from. What are the sources of income right now? My friend Bob Allen did a great set of tapes called Multiple Streams of Income. If you only have one source of income, that's called a job, which is an acronym I say means Just Over Broke. When we wrote *Chicken Soup for the Soul,* Jack Canfield and I were both speakers. You always have to focus on doing your best for your main business, but then start writing down what you want to be your multiple sources of income.

I read the biographies of Steven Spielberg and George Lucas. Both of them were licensing. Jack and I got into licensing and one of our original licenses was greeting cards. Today, the *Chicken Soup for the Soul*-branded products have accounted for over $2 billion in total retail sales worldwide in the past twenty years. In additional producing many products in-house, we operate an active trademark licensing program. We continuously monitor licensed products to ensure that they are in line with our primary goal: to share happiness, inspiration, and wellness through everything we do.

I'm asking you to write down some possible multiple sources of income. What are the ten additional income sources you can create? Notice the word "create." I don't want you to take a job. I want you to create things out of that wonderfully abundant, fertile imagination that you have. If you don't see yourself right now as having multiple streams of income, just embrace it as an idea; write it down as a goal. We'll discuss this more in an upcoming chapter.

Write down whether you want two or three other sources of income. When you get two or three, others will emerge and you can increase the number to 10, 20, 50, or 100. Then I want you to inspire other people to do that. Maybe share this book with somebody so you can talk about it heart to heart, soul to soul, mind to mind.

PREPARING FOR CHANGE

Now I want you to consider creating for yourself a real MBA—a Massive Bank Account. Ask yourself the following questions:

- What changes do you anticipate might affect your financial position?

- What do you need to do to prepare for those changes?

- Do you have sufficient health and life insurance?

- Do you have sufficient disability insurance? Unfortunately, the chances of becoming disabled is way higher than dying early, so you have to have it.

- Are your assets sufficiently diversified so you can survive any kind of unpleasant financial surprise that may be created by the problems of the past few years? You ought to have some money in: real estate; investments; the Internet; marketing; and you ought to create some passive income possibilities.

Do you want to get to where you're working and serving because you *want* to? Wouldn't it be nice if you go to work and you feel free, joyous, and inspired. When I interviewed Mother Teresa, she said she puts everybody on probation. Everyone from around the world who comes to Calcutta, India, to work with her has to have the spirit of joy. When you're in a spirit of joy, you are a money attractor. You attract possibilities and opportunities that don't come to people who are negative. Earl Nightingale in one of the early sets of tapes that lead the field said more jobs are ruined and more marriages are destroyed by a bad attitude than any other single thing. I'm sure that's true. When you passionately love what you're doing, money finds a way to find you. Peter J. Daniels is one of my friends from Adelaide, Australia, and one of the richest industrialists in the world. He was a board member of Mother Teresa's and he told me that when she died, her ministry, Missionaries of Charity Sisters, was grossing more than $500 million per year and had four Lear jets. See what I mean? Even someone this self-sacrificially serving needs to have a war chest.

If you've never written down how much you want to have in your war chest, now's the time to do it.

YOUR NET WORTH

Next, calculate your net worth purely in terms of dollars and cents. Your net worth is your assets minus your liabilities. How much do you have left after you've subtracted what you owe. Once you've created an accurate picture your financial landscape, it's easy to look at the number which is your financial net worth. The idea of your financial net worth as it exists today is a good transition point for starting to look at your situation in larger terms. In the world today, value is determined not only by what you have right now but also by what you can give in the future.

Cavett Robert always said your future earning power is probably the most important thing you have after your family and your spiritual values. My great and inspiring teacher for seven years Bucky Fuller said, "Real wealth, RW, equals ideas plus energy. Ideas you can only learn more. Energy only gets recycled and revamped." So we're in the greatest sharing time of ideas in this book because as I share the best, the brightest, and the wisest ideas with you, it doesn't take anything from me. It's like the metaphor discussed earlier. When you light your candle from mine, it didn't take anything away from mine, but actually makes the world fourfold brighter. Same thing here about ideas and energy.

An idea from one mind to another mind may be invested better and multiplied more exponentially in a second mind than in the first. When I heard Cavett Robert talk about multi-authored books, I didn't know that I would become one of the world's best-selling authors. You just don't know what can happen! You're investing your learning time right here gathering new ideas, new possibilities, new probabilities for a future energy that can only be transformed and reused. Therefore, your real wealth is about to boom.

If anyone asks me how business is, my philosophy and affirmation is to say, "Business is booming!" In fact it's always booming for someone, somewhere, somehow, sometime, somehow. Let that someone be you. Nurture it, expect it, anticipate it, and have a vision that it's going to be yours; and it'll be the trigger and the anchor thought to make you richer, brighter, more exciting, and have a more meaningful tomorrow.

Let's look at what you can do right now to make sure your net worth is where it needs to be. You reach this new point in your life. I'm not limiting this discussion to the amounts that can be quantified in terms of mutual funds, your pension, profit sharing, and investments. That kind of net worth certainly is important; but let's widen the scope now to include a larger definition of assets and liabilities. What are your most important assets in making your dreams happen? All you need are two things—desire and commitment. Once you have the desire and you have your dream and you have it pictured, all you need is one key contact and voila! you're going to get a fortune. After that you can borrow everything else—talent, wherewithal, ideas, networks of connections, direct mail, mentors, resource skills, and relationships that you didn't know you can have. In fact, everyone who's ever created wealth did just that.

Your intangible wealth—desire and commitment—makes your imagination, ambition, energy, creativity, and possibility bloom. They convert into the tangible asset called real estate, intellectual property, stocks, bonds, a portfolio, money in whatever form called your financial portfolio. So remember this, it's your intangibles that make the tangible. We're working on your intangible. We're talking about how to decorate the home entertainment center called your mind with those intangibles. In his classic book *Think and Grow Rich,* Napoleon Hill goes through thirteen principles, all of which are intangibles that become tangible.

Everyone says, "Show me your riches." Twenty or thirty years ago I couldn't prove to you that my intangibles would become tangible, but I could promise that I could perform and deliver. Maybe you don't think you have what it takes. You do! I want to get inside you and stimulate you to awaken your confidence. There are too many valuable resources, too much talent within you to let it go to waste.

Spiritually, it violates spirit if you bury it. You're called wicked and slothful; but if you multiply it, you're called good and faithful. I want you to be good and faithful and multiply at levels you don't even know you can right now.

RETURN ON LIFE

All this leads to a very important point. There's a lot of information out there about the costs of retirement and what your net worth needs to be to sustain the lifestyle you want. There's a newer and broader definition of net worth that pertains to how you really want to invest the rest of your life. In business it's called ROI, return on investment. What we're talking about here is return on life. When it's over and you have those snapshots to look back at, what do you see? How valuable was your life? How good were the relationships? Were they so deep and meaningful and pregnant with possibility that the hinges of the relationship never rusted? Rather they became mightier; and every time you synchronized in time and space with that person you had a new excitement glowing.

Why not have a whole set of relationships like that to make your life more valuable and meaningful? Create memories that you want to create for yourself your family and your team. Like my hero Bob Hope sang, "Thanks for the memories" that he made his archetypal song. How clear are your dreams and focus? What are the tools you're learning to use to make it happen.

You start to do conceptually what is going to become the reality in your future. Are you cultivating million-dollar ideas? Have you written down at least one of your 101 goals such as *I'm going to have a million dollar* idea. As that goal permeates, penetrates, and fills the inner space of your mind, voila! It will pop out of your head like bread out of a toaster in the morning for breakfast.

Is it hard to have a million dollar idea? No. It's just like when Jack and I wanted the ideal title for the book, which he was going to call Happy Little Stories. We used the work of Erick Erickson, a psychiatrist and hypnotherapist. He said, "Go into deep meditation and say 400 times in a row, 'Mega best-selling title, mega best-selling title, mega best-selling title,' and then give yourself a thought command what time you're going wake up with the answer." At four o'clock in the morning, Jack woke up and came up with the title *Chicken Soup for the Soul.* He woke up his wife, called me, and my wife said, "this better be good." Well, I got goose bumps. He got goose bumps, we all got goose bumps.

Now when we went to sell it, remember I told you every one rejected us. They couldn't see it. But it doesn't matter if anyone else can see the truth of your million dollar idea. What matters is that *you* make the decision in your subconscious, and the world and the universe will make the provision. But you have to keep saying yes to yourself because every idea is stillborn. So you have to say yes to it, nurture it, cultivate it, and then get others who are like-minded to say yes to it.

TO MAKE A MILLION DOLLARS

To make a million dollars, you should apply Occam's razor, which is, according to the dictionary: "a scientific and philosophical rule that entities should not be multiplied unnecessarily which is interpreted as requiring that the simplest of competing theories be preferred to the more complex or that explanations of unknown phenomena be sought first in terms of known quantities." In other words, use the simplest, the best, the easiest, and the fastest route to accomplish a goal.

For example, when Bob Allen and I put together that little mega mastermind dream team of forty of the best marketing minds, I asked our friend Brian Tracy, "If one of your four kid's life depended on it, how would you pre-sell one million copies of the book."

Brian said immediately, "Occam's razor."

"What does that mean?" I asked. Well, we knew that was to do it the fastest, simplest, best, and easiest way. But I said, "What way would that be, Brian?"

"To find someone to buy one million books," he said.

At first we all laughed. However, the more we explored the idea, the closer we came to figuring out how to implement it and the more possible the impossible seemed. With a mastermind team, you cultivate miracles. Brian challenged us and that's what a mastermind is all about. It's about challenging you. Dr. Ken Blanchard said the way you challenge somebody is to say, "You're better than that; you can do more than that; your thinking can cultivate more."

Marketing and packaging is 90 percent of success in the United States. We're the world's leader in marketing our talent, services, products, personality, and information. When talking about wealth building, that may mean that you have to build some new skills. I want you to write as one of your goals the skills that you need. They're going to be breakthrough skills that are going to challenge you and change your life. And we need to pick up new skills every year. You're not supposed to learn something once and do it for the next 30, 40, 50 years.

One of the businesses you ought to consider is writing—because everyone has information they can market. You know more about something than anyone else. And if you worked hard to find that information, somebody else is willing to pay you for it. That's one of the ways for you to make money.

Some say they're not capable of writing a book. My friend Cindy Cashman said she couldn't write a book—but she said she could write a title. And the title was so humorous and uplifting and joyful: *Everything Men Know about Women.* And when you open the book, the pages were blank! The first year, she made $4 million selling a blank book because every woman didn't buy one, they bought five or ten. She gave me one to "read," and I thought it was the funniest thing I've ever seen.

You never have a money crisis. You only have an idea crisis. Ideas attract money. Most say, "Well, if I had money then I'd have ideas." That's not the way it works, and is why you have to have your journal to sculpt in it. Hopefully you will write down ideas every day as you capture your ideas. Earl Nightingale said ideas are like wet, slippery fish you got to gaff them and hook them when they're loose and out and about. As you capture and write down those ideas, more and more ideas will inflow you, and then you'll start to overflow with the ideas. You will want to share them with people. Some will hold you accountable, asking you, "Have you done what you said you're going to do yet?" Then you will get about your business and get results.

When you get the right idea, you're going to have more right ideas. So write down all those ideas and then use Occam's razor. Figure out how to do the big ideas, the glowing ideas, the ideas that have some verve and vitality, and sex appeal. Figure out your dream—something about which you can say, "This is what I really want to do."

IDEAS ARE THE SOURCE

Ideas are the source of everything. God said in the beginning was the word. Best understood: in the beginning was the idea, the concept, the thought. Our words and ideas are forever taking form. *Think and Grow Rich's* first principle is thoughts or things. It's an irrefutable principle; you can direct your thinking and lead your life to wherever you want it to go. It doesn't matter what you haven't done, haven't said, haven't thought, haven't felt. Right now get positive and get permanent in your ideas. Get solid with the fact that you're going to create what you want.

When you tell yourself that problems are good, it converts your 18 billion brain cells and you can take adversity and turn it into an asset. You can create stuff that you didn't know you could create, and you can have a breakthrough Pygmalion effect in your life, going from low self-esteem to high self-esteem, from no fulfillment to high self-fulfillment, where you are writing your own self-fulfilling prophecy.

I am excited about all the possibilities, because I want to end joblessness. When I was unemployed, I felt trashed. And now I know for a fact that each millionaire creates ten new jobs and each billionaire creates ten thousand new jobs. And if we create one million millionaires and four hundred billionaires that's fourteen million new jobs in the United States. Then we can extend that around the world and we can end unemployment. We can enfranchise the two billion people who are disenfranchised.

That would be so great—and we could do it without violating any cultures. It's a great idea; it's a grand idea; it's a big idea; it's idealistic; but for the first time in history, it's doable, it's possible. That's what I'm saying about your wealth—have big ideas that excite all of your eighteen billion brain cells to come to work at a new velocity. I want you to think big, achieve big, and create big wealth. I want you to be able to enjoy the good things that work brings to you—and as importantly, I want you to contribute greatly and leave a legacy that lasts and perpetuates itself.

FUNDAMENTAL ABUNDANCE

I think fundamental abundance is available for every person. It is the truth of every spiritual system and the oldest spiritual literature on the planet. The first literature written 6,000 years ago is The Upanishads, and the first line says, "Out of abundance he took abundance and still abundance remained." We can grow enough food to feed everyone, but we can only do all those things if we have enough wealth to do it.

When I wrote the *Chicken Soup for the Soul* cookbook, I didn't do it because I wanted to do it but because Sol Price came to us and said, "You're selling twenty thousand books a week through Costco Price Club, and we want you to do a cookbook." I said, "Sol, Jack and I don't do cookbooks." He said, "Our first order is a quarter million." I said, "Sol, we can do a cookbook."

So, we met with the top female cookbook writer. Two years in a row she was a cookbook lady of the year award winner. That's what I mean about building your wealth—you have to build new teams and new esteem. We worked with Diana von Welanetz Wentworth and we built this new idea. The book was successful because I believe that if you want more, you have to be charitable. We've tithed every one of our *Chicken Soup for the Soul* books; and I think that is one of the major pieces that has made our book series a rocking success.

In the cookbook I wrote, "Let's feed LA on Turkey Day." We looked around at the charities that could do the biggest, the best, and the grandest job. We chose the Union Rescue Mission in LA to help us. President of the Mission, Warren Currie, is the Mother Teresa of LA. His energetic presence and commitment makes tears well up in your eyes. He said, "What do you boys want to do?" We told him that with Diana we wanted to feed LA on Turkey Day and we would pay for it. We ultimately had to turn down 428 people who wanted to contribute to feeding and taking care of the people. *USA Today* wrote a front-page article about it because we did what we said we would do.

You don't do the wealth for yourself alone—wealth alone isn't enough. You can do wealth and source and serve great masses of people at levels you can't even imagine right now. All I'm asking you to do is just get started. Decide in favor of yourself. Write down, "I'm happy that I'm going to be an enlightened millionaire and I'm going to be a massively big contributor in ways I never thought I could do before." Your decision is going to amaze, excite and delight you because it will come to pass.

CHAPTER 5

THE FUN FACTOR

One of the most neglected elements in all the areas of personal development is the fun factor. It doesn't matter how much you believe in your head that you want to make positive changes. And it doesn't matter how much you feel it in your heart. Unless there are some moment-to-moment rewards built into the process, your motivation will erode over time— it'll go dead or go into dread. In other words, you have to be doing something that has fun in it!

It's important to make your work, work-play, and that's especially true as we get older. Having fun is what makes our heart sing. It puts the wind beneath our wings and fun is the best part when it's shared—it multiplies enjoyment. Some years ago an amazing study was done on the number of times that people laugh in different stages of their lives. Kids who are two or three years old laugh literally hundreds of times during the course of day. They fall over and they laugh, they giggle when the milk spills.

Between ages of 3 and 70, though, there are young people who are too serious for their own good. There are older people who still love and laugh, but as people get older, studies have shown that laughter frequency starts to diminish. Unfortunately, by the time some people reach their seventh decade of life, they have become so unaccustomed to laughing that the muscles in their face can't perform or function physically. They couldn't laugh if they wanted to.

Something very similar happens to some people's personalities. They become inflexible, rigid and stiff, stuck in their ways, and begin to think the world is going to the dogs. It's been true since ancient times. No doubt you've seen quotations written over the centuries complaining about the terrible state of things. What can we do to ward off pessimism and help people be kids again so they exude and bubble over with the effervescence of joy and have fun laughing and smiling? It's not just for commercials like McDonald's that says, "We love to see you smile." I think everybody loves to see other people smile, and laughter is one of the best ways to start a chain reaction of happiness.

Misery is a decision you *don't* have to make. You can decide to laugh, love, enjoy life, and be radiantly, exuberantly happy. You *are* the party. When you have a party inside, the party shows up outside. My friend Dr. Wayne Dyer says if you squeeze an orange, what kind of juice comes out? Orange juice. But if you get squeezed and anger comes out, it's because anger is inside. If you get squeezed and laughter comes out, it's because you've put laughter inside.

DECORATE YOUR MIND

In this chapter you will learn how to put laughter inside your own self-created home entertainment center called your mind.

How are you decorating it? Why not decorate it with happy pictures, cartoons, jokes, humor, things that uplift you and exalt you! I urge you to be much more proactive about creating a place in your mind of pure joy, pure happiness, and pure fun.

What does that involve? What does it mean to be *at* fun and *in* fun? To me, it's any self-fulfilling activity that does not depend on a particular outcome. It's not about winning or losing. It's not about making a deadline. It's about going beyond all those categories and making something happen that is fun, for the sake of fun.

Why not decide to look at life and say, "I'm going to have fun having fun!" In the morning before you get out of bed visualize yourself sparkling, radiant. See the reaction of the world when they see you as a joyful, exciting individual. A mailman said, "I never know how I feel until I've looked in the eyes of three other people." Well, if you're the one who is creating that echo effect, the world's response to your enthusiasm is going to be one of enjoyment, smiles, and warmth. You can exude a radiance of joy that will multiply and return to you magnetized and magnified, bringing joy to each and every situation.

Years ago, my friend and Horatio Alger colleague and the world's top pediatric neurosurgeon Dr. Ben Carson said he chose to be in a spirit of joy and share it with his patients and colleagues. As a youngster, Ben, his mother, and brother were very poor and living in Detroit. In third grade Ben was considered a slow learner. His mother, however, was very loving and always saw more in Ben and his brother than they saw in themselves. She told Ben that every day he was to go to the library, check out a book, read the book, and write a book report that she would read. After one year of reading and then writing a book report every day for his mother, who was totally illiterate but he didn't know that, he advanced from the bottom of his academic class to the very top of the class.

In his professional career, Ben achieved the impossible when in 1987 he successfully separated conjoined twins. He pioneered the first successful neurosurgical procedure on a fetus inside the womb and became the youngest chief of pediatric neurosurgery at age 33. In 2008, he was awarded the Presidential Medal of Freedom, the highest civilian award in the United States. He retired from medicine in 2013 and is currently the United States Secretary of Housing and Urban Development. His mother, Sonya Carson, came from an impoverished background and had only a third-grade education, yet she left a great legacy. Ben says of her, "If anyone had a reason to make excuses, it was her, but she absolutely refused to be a victim and would not permit us to develop the victim mentality either." Ben's a radiant being who inspires joy in everyone around him. His story and the influence of his mother is told in the book and movie, *Gifted Hands.*

The next example is Picasso. Why did he live to be 94 years old and still have a twinkle in his spirit? It's said that he clicked his heels every day when he walked down the hall. As a matter of fact, why do so many painters not only live into their 90s but continue to be productive to the end of their lives? I think it's related to the fact that what they do is basically a lot of fun. They're in their art form, which is what I'm asking you to do. Figure out what your art form is and then manifest it. After all, they're doing exactly what little kids do and have fun doing.

An artist may have more talent, discipline, and ability than a kindergartner, but the activity is basically the same. They get to make a mess. They get to play. They get to show off their talent. And instead of their work-play hanging on a refrigerator, they receive real recognition. It hangs in museums and art galleries and in some of the finest homes and businesses in the world.

Why not adorn the world with *your* artwork—whatever is your passion. Picasso was always on the leading edge of things; he put masks on faces, drew funny animals, sculpted things. His whole life he never stopped doing the things that he did when he was a little kid. He never stopped having fun. Picasso was a reductionist, always trying to do everything in the most economical of all ways. He was considered by *The Guinness Book of World Records.* to be the world's most productive artist.

It's no coincidence that someone who is having so much fun is also very successful. Nor is it a coincidence that although Picasso almost casually produced works that sold for a great deal of money, his painting talent came through his soul, that came through his spirit; and he had an incredible sense of fun while he was doing it.

WHALING WALLS

The new Picasso of our times is a friend of mine, Robert Wyland. He painted 100 Whaling Walls—very large outdoor murals of life-size humpback whales and other sea life—that took thirty years, in thirteen countries and four continents. From Laguna Beach, *California Grey Whale and Calf* to painting with children in Kuala Lumpur, Malaysia, to Beijing, China, and Key West Florida, he had two purposes in mind when beginning this work-play. One is to make sure everybody in the world starts paying attention to keeping the oceans clean. When we were diving together and in O'ahu, Hawaii, we saw 400-year old turtles under the sea and all of them had cancer eroding their faces. When we surfaced, we said, "This has to change." We joined our talents.

His 100th mural was painted in advance of the 2008 summer Olympic Games in China. The mural spanned almost two miles with more than 100 giant canvasses creating a "Great Green Wall of China." Wyland and thousands of children from around the world collaborated to paint the world's aquatic habitats and their inhabitants—manatees, sea turtles, bald eagles, beavers—wildlife found in their home countries. Why did we do that? Because for us it's fun. In 2012, we published *Chicken Soup for the Ocean Lover's Soul,* featuring Wyland artwork "to open the heart and rekindle the spirit."

The highest form of fun as far as I'm concerned is good thinking. Are you able to do good thinking? Yes. This whole book is dedicated to is waking you up, getting rid of the cobwebs, getting you to go to some of the recesses of that untapped potential in you. It's what Russell Conwell calls *Acres of Diamonds* in that classic book. You need to go deep because you have more acres of diamonds in your mind. Earl Nightingale said you have more acres of diamonds in your mind than have ever been mined from any gold field in the world.

Educational Ecstasy

We're leveraging abundance into the future. We're leveraging thinking; and when you leverage thinking, we decide to make thinking fun. The trouble with today's education is instead of being what George Leonard wrote about in his book *Education and Ecstasy,* we've made it educational drudgery. Most think, *I gotta go to school and I hate it.* I've done everything I could to make sure my kids have educational fun going through their life.

I audited six kindergarten classes, and one teacher was having fun in her classroom. She still loved teaching. Hang out with people who are having fun in their art form. This lady made education ecstasy. I went into her kindergarten class and sat there and listened while she sang to the students. She spoke to them multilingually. And when she was trying to teach something of importance and impact, she whispered in one kid's ear and what she said was passed along to all of the 20 or 30 kids who were in her classroom. The last one said exactly what she said, which was amazing to me. Adults can't do that.

When she had them do the alphabet kinesthetically, I knew this was a homerun teacher. She had the kids do the whole alphabet with their physical bodies. They stood up and said, "This is a Y," as they held their hands high and spread outward. Then a T and an X. She had the students roll up on the floor like a Q. It was a cutest thing I think I've ever seen. If we make education fun, it becomes fun.

I taught my daughters not to take a class unless they audit the teacher. Don't take a class because you need an economics class. Choose a class with the greatest economic teacher.

There's no topic that can't be fun. When I was a freshman in college, before I really applied this to myself, I failed chemistry. I retook the class and earned an A-plus. Why? Because I had a teacher to taught me the architecture of the molecule, how to get inside the subject. I ended up doing really well in school because once I picked the teacher who had fun teaching the subject, I was inspired; I had fun.

What am I saying? Everything has to be taught. Some things can be *caught* but they're caught and taught by a great and inspiring teacher who is having fun. I want you to have fun having fun. I want you to decide in favor of yourself and decide that you're going to hang around people who are fun. Be decisive, take action, and do what no one's ever done before.

THE RIGHT DIRECTION

The following are some of the things I'd like you to do for fun, to think about, and a few questions to get you headed in the right direction, if you're ready. And if you've read this, far I'm convinced you're deeply and profoundly ready.

When was…

When was the last time you subscribed to a new magazine—a magazine that you're excited to read, a magazine that you rip the plastic off and start to delve into it immediately? When's the last time you went to the library? When was the last time you ate at a new restaurant? Step out and do something different and make it fun.

When was…

When was the last time you read an out-of-town newspaper? When you read another regional, city, or foreign paper, it opens different thoughts in your mind—you're exposed to different points of view of the area and the world. Did you know that *Time* magazine in foreign countries is different from the *Time* magazine in the US? And when was the last time you explored different parts of your region, city, or state? Exploring with a variety of people also brings different perspectives about topics you may have never considered.

When was...

When was the last time you attended a religious service other than your own? One of the many churches that we attend is in Los Angeles, Agape. I brought the second in command to Sai Baba, an Indian spiritual master, to talk at that church and it was absolutely packed. If you're a Christian, why shouldn't your church invite a Jewish person to come and speak, or a Hindu or Muslim. Different points of view prompt you to think in new ways. You don't have to abandon your own beliefs to hear about others, and it may even prove to solidify what you believe.

When was...

When was the last time you made a new friend or friends? Every friend you meet opens you up to a whole new category of about 250 other people you could meet. It's not only who you know, but who you know that they know and who they know, etc. You will read more about connections later in the book.

When was...

When was the last time you laughed so hard you cried? Or you laughed so hard your stomach hurt? Or you laughed so hard that you had to massage your jaw because of the pain. Do you have at least one friend in your coterie of friends who when you're feeling trashed you can call any time of day or night? Do you have someone who will pick you up and perk you up?

When was...

What was the last time you joined a new organization that would revitalize your thinking? Or did something totally out of character that would help you grow and expand?

When was...

When was the last time you played with a child and became not childish but childlike? Maybe you built a sand-castle with your children or sat swinging at the playground with a neighborhood youngster. Maybe you enjoyed a game of Monopoly or read a children's book with a child's imagination and saw how great it was.

When was...

When was the last time you learned a foreign language? Right now I'm learning another foreign language via a CD in my car. Why not learn languages constantly? If you have kids and grandkids, my recommendation is to have them learn multiple languages before they're twelve years old, when it's easiest. But if you tell yourself that it's easy at any stage to have fun learning a language, you can do it.

When was...

When was the last time you bought somebody a gift for no reason and you didn't have to explain it to yourself or anyone else? You just bought the gift because you knew it to be the right thing for another person.

When was...

When's the last time you did volunteer work of any kind? And if you are writing your goals, one of your goals should be: what are the ten kinds of volunteer work that I want to do that no one's ever done before that will make everybody better off.

When was...

When was the last time you did something that you used to do all the time and had fun doing it? Maybe if you scuba dive and haven't for a while, maybe you need to do that. Maybe if you haven't parachuted in a while, you may want to do that. President George H. W. Bush skydived from a plane to celebrate his 90th birthday. Should we become agents of break-through in life? Yes!

HAVE FUN HAVING FUN

Whatever you do, be aware of the tendency that exists in many people as they get older to get grumpier and complain more. It's the Scrooge syndrome. No doubt you read Dickens' book and watched the movie. When you start to have those feelings, don't trust them. They're not the truth of who you are. Resist them, because inside you is an eternally young person. You own the fountain of youth inside you. And it's turned on and turned up by the amount of fun you decide to have. You have to decide to have fun having fun.

Turn upside down the old direction and become the new you. It's like the hourglass you turn upside down to bring your dreams into the real world. Never lose the capacity to have fun. On the other hand your dreams are waiting for you. It's like the character Kevin Costner played in the movie *Field of Dreams.* He visualized what could happen and then he morphed his little farm into a field of dreams—that is now the most visited place in all of Iowa. He had his field of dreams; and he knew that if he built on it, it would come true.

Likewise, if you build in yourself fun having fun, the world will come to dance at your feet. It's not just for Victor Borge to have fun. He was a Danish pianist, conductor, songwriter, actor, and humorist who had fun everywhere he went. You and I too can have fun everywhere we go, with everyone we meet— when we decide to have fun having fun.

CHAPTER 6

CONNECTIONS COUNT

It's been said that life at first is a process of expansion; and later on in life it's a process of contraction. It's a simple enough concept to understand when we're young in the world and our own capabilities are getting bigger. Then as we become older, we reverse the process; we start to contract. It's definitely a process you want to resist, especially as it pertains to the number of people in your life and the quality of your relationships.

To stay young and prosper, you have to keep cultivating young friends. You have to cultivate your wealth and your health—and you have to cultivate more and more purposes to be on purpose about.

When we study the development of any great idea, we invariably find that it didn't happen in a vacuum. When it seemed that only one person was involved, it became obvious that others were always present to provide information, inspiration, and support. An example is Edwin Land. One day he brought pictures home that he had picked up at the local store. He showed them to his 5-year-old son who said something like, "Daddy, why can't we get pictures right away? Why do we have to wait a week?" That got Land thinking and masterminding with his son, and voila! in one year that one great idea became the first Polaroid camera, which turned into a multibillion dollar company.

Often a great idea has remained dormant in the mind of a given individual until contact with someone else triggers it and brings it into realization. It is impossible to predict that the new person might be the catalyst to galvanize the idea and make it a reality for the rest of us.

In business, there are three parts: innovation, optimization, and acceleration. Let's look at each. Innovation is always intrinsically messy. One of my three favorite lines in the Bible is in Proverbs where it says the only clean barn is an empty barn. Meaning, if you have stacked innovation, you can have a messy barn. You're going to have some horse poop there, so to speak. No matter what you're going to do, to be successful, you have to do more of it in less time and faster and better, and get better results in your tomorrow than you did in your yesterday or even that you're getting today. How are you going to do that? You can do it if you're networking with people who are true to their heart and true to innovation, no matter when they do it in their lives.

Sir Alexander Fleming, for example, was a physician in his late 40s when he was researching the growth of bacteria. He happened to leave a dish on a windowsill in the lab and more or less forgot about it. Eventually he probably would have just washed it out and put it away. But a friend who happened to be visiting pointed out the mold that had developed in the dish and had killed the surrounding bacteria. Fleming immediately realized the significance of what had happened and this was the discovery of penicillin that revolutionized the treatment of disease. If Fleming had been alone in his laboratory, he most likely would have never noticed the mold.

We have an archetypal story about a British gentleman who takes his 12-year-old to Scotland, and the son goes swimming alone. All sudden he starts to drown, he's bobbing up and down and yelling, "Help, help, help!" A young farm boy dives in and saves his life. The next day the English gentleman comes and says to the young farm boy, "What do you want to be when you grow up?" The boy says, "I want to grow up to become a great physician and a great scientist. But my parents are poor and I don't have any money." The gentleman said, "Because you saved my son's life, I'll send you through school as long as you earn good grades."

We don't know when one person's life is going to connect with another. You can't even predict it. All you can do is write it into your diary and your goal journal that in the future you will have lots and lots of friends. And write what kind of friends you want to have, what they ideally would be like. Write what your conversations will be like.

INVISIBLE NETWORK OF PEOPLE

In the book *Think and Grow Rich*, when Napoleon Hill didn't have anybody rich to hang out with or anyone to support him, he created an invisible network of people. When I was bankrupt and upside down financially, I was eating peanut butter until my tongue stuck to the roof of my mouth. I was feeling totally out of it. Yet when I read that about Hill, I thought, *If I don't have my ideal dream team, I can still have an imaginary dream team like Hill.* From that moment, I had on my mental, invisible mastermind team Walt Disney who would tell me things that I put into my talks. And Abe Lincoln would with wisdom. John Kennedy was part of my mental, invisible mastermind team too.

So if you don't have who you want right now in your life, you can create him and her in your imagination. That's the good news.

There's a clear similarity between the development of thinking capacity of the human brain and development of creative potential of society as a whole—both depend on the transformation of a large group of isolated entities into an interconnected network of communication cooperation. We call it co-op-petition where competitors come together and create something brand-new.

In the first three years of life, individual neurons in the brain are connected to one another and the extent to which this happens seems to determine the cognitive power of the individual. The amount of stimulation that a child receives determines the extent to which brain cells connect.

All studies show that the more brain cells used, the more exposure in a positive way, the more colors, interaction, and stimulation, the better. Positive stimuli is great for brain development.

I studied with Dr. Jean Houston, the godmother of the whole human potential movement. She worked with thirty-five governments around the world. We know that human potential can happen at any time, when you have the requisite stimulus, and become realization that you can't believe. I've watched Dr. Houston at a seminar on potential take a Catholic nun who had no art ability and she drew a leaf. I've seen her trance-state an individual who can't play the piano and get into the ethos of being Mozart or Beethoven. A few minutes later, the person is playing rudimentary, unpublished works by, let's say, Mozart.

All of us are connected. In India they call it the Akashic records, the infinite knowingness. I believe that if we stay connected and get with the right people, there's probably no limitation to what we can do. There are somebodies out there who have every talent and answer for every question you have. There are people who can see more in you than what you can see. That's why you have to stay connected, get connected, maximize your exposure, and maximize your possibilities.

COMMUNICATION REVOLUTION

In a similar way, it's clear that individual members of our society and of the world as a whole are more interconnected. This is the result of the information communication revolution and I think we're actually going into the age of wisdom. I think this book is sort of the entryway into that age because we have more information than we know how to handle and more communication than we can possibly process. If we really go to our wiser self, our higher self, our better self, the potential self with the blueprint of us as the best we can be, then we take all the deadlines off our dreams and start to realize and take advantage of and leverage ourselves forward.

This involves both high tech and low tech approaches. For instance, you don't need a computer or a smart phone to meet at least one new person every day. Why not make it a goal to meet one new person every day no matter what. I had a great 80-year-old friend in a network-marketing business. His goal was always to meet one new person every day. If he didn't meet one on Monday, on Tuesday he had to meet two, and on Wednesday three. Why don't you do that? I believe that the person with the biggest list of contacts wins.

In our millionaire training, I'm suggesting you meet one new millionaire a month, then two a week, and then two a day. Ask him or her, "How did you make your million? How do you recommend I make my million? If you were me, what would you do to make a million? Do you have any project that you think we could monetize, million-ize, and is there anything I could do with you to help realize that project?" It's amazing what will happen—why not decide to do it, starting sooner than later?

It is essential that you get wired into the whole world of the Internet and high communication.

The more you learn, the more you earn. When you understand the importance of getting and staying connected and you've identified both the high and low tech means of doing so, you've already answered some of the all-important questions. For example, who should I stay connected with?

In marketing we say you ought to stay in touch with the people on your contact list seven times. If you can do it physically, that's great. Or by letter, email, telephone, or tell another person. The point is, you want to have a list of 200 influential, powerful, prestigious people with whom you want to work, play, grow, expand, travel, and do business.

Joe Girard, the world's greatest car salesman, said that he knew that everyone he sold a car to had a little diary, or address book at home of about 250 people they know and love and respect and admire and appreciate. So he said to each of the buyers, "I want you to be my bird dog. I'll give you twenty five dollars for everyone who comes in here and buys a car from me." He sold more than 1,425 cars in one year and 13,000 cars in ten years. How? One reason was his bird dog tactic and another was that he wrote a thank-you note to everyone who bought a car from him.

NETWORKING SAVVY

In all the books I sign for youngsters, I always write, "I like you," which was inspired by my friend Joe Girard. Why? Because most of us need somebody else to validate our self-worthiness, especially when you're young, especially when you're not sure of yourself. Everyone has some issue going on and it's hard for most people to just walk up to someone and say hi. One time in Hawaii our little daughter strolled over to another kid on the beach and said, "Hi, I'm Melanie. Can we play?" And she just started playing with this kid. It was amazing.

Most people aren't that outgoing. Most are going to meet somebody sitting in an airplane or bus. There we usually say, "How do you like the food," or something neutral and simple like, "Hi, I'm Joe, do you mind if we talk?" Then we ask questions like, "Where are you from? What's your business? What do you do for fun? What are your hobbies?"

A few people won't want to talk to you; but more often than not, people want to talk because they want to relate, interact, get to know you, and pass the time. I recommend you meet them, then make sure you put their name and other information in your contact list. You may even want to write notes about the person. And if you are really smart, you put all the information you know about the person into your daily journal. Days, weeks, or even months or years later, you may find a link to this person who holds the key to a great venture. This is how you get to be good at networking.

In an earlier chapter I suggested that you do something a little uncomfortable for you that makes you grow. As Ray Kroc said, "If you're green, you're growing. If you're ripe, you rot; and if you're blue, you're through." Presidential candidates and wannabe presidential candidates have to glad-hand, shake hands, smile and talk to a lot of people and make them feel instantaneously comfortable with themselves. Most of them become master networkers. They have an above average hand-shake and a mighty gaze.

As a speaker, I have to shake hands with a lot of people before I go to the platform. I get to meet whoever has hired me, plus all the top people in that company, and each one has something to say. As an author, when I start signing books after the presentation, an amazing thing happens. When they ask me to sign their books, in thirty seconds they expect to tell me their biggest, deepest, most profound problem. Usually the ones with tears in their eyes say, "Can I take you over to my office...I want to tell you something." They really expect me to have the answer. And while my prayers are that I always have the answer, I don't know that I will.

The point is, most people need somebody to talk to; and the value here is be a good listener, an active listener. We have two eyes and two ears, so we're supposed to listen twice as much as we talk. When you take time to listen, your value exponentially goes up in their mind.

My cliché is, when your network goes up, your net worth goes up. So, one of the books you have to read to build your network is the classic by Dale Carnegie, *How to Win Friends and Influence People.* What he learned a long time ago is that when you keep asking people questions about what interests them, which are nonjudgmental and nonintimidating, they open up like an ever-flowering lotus. Then at the end of the conversation they'll say you're the best conversationalist in the world. Yet you haven't said anything; all you did was ask them about themselves and listen.

Everybody is fascinating to me, so I usually ask, "Do you mind if I take notes?" I encourage you to do that too because your value will grow exponentially and increase as you become an active grower of your contact list. It's not only who *you* know and who *they* know, but who *you* know that *they* know that matters.

The other part is who knows you. One of my early mentors said, "If they don't hire you to speak, they won't see you and can't recommend you. They can't rehire you, and they can't refer you." It's the same in about every business. If they don't know you, they can't use you. You have to broadcast yourself by choosing to network to build your net worth.

TURN OFF TOXIC TALK

The only part of the network you want to stay away from is toxic people. You know, the people who brighten up a whole room when they walk *out* of it. I remember back when I was just starting my speaking career and I was talking at a Rotary Club meeting. Before my presentation, all I did was innocently ask a guy how business was. Well, it was 1974 when the market had just trashed and crashed. This guy proceeded to bombard me with negativity. I didn't know then how to resist toxic talk and I started believing what he was saying. Consequently, when I got up to talk, the wind had been taken out of my wings and out of my sails, so to speak. I was suffering from the doldrums up there, crashing and burning.

Rather than spend any time at all with toxic people, make a list of all the people you want to meet and greet. I'm going to ask you to go one step further. Go through all your favorite magazines—don't do this with library's or your dentist's magazines—cut out the pictures of all the people you want to meet. Put them in your daily journal or make a special journal for the photos and write what it is about the person that intrigues you.

SEE WHAT YOU WANT

I have a great friend who has made himself exceedingly successful. His name is John Assaraf. I first met him in Indianapolis and heard his story. He was born in Tel Aviv and he and his parents emigrated to Montreal, Canada. He sold real estate in Canada did an exceedingly good job, making what he thought was the fortune of all fortunes—$180,000. So he took off the next 18 months and traveled around the world. When he returned, he was still in his early 20s and decided he wanted to own a RE/MAX real estate franchise. Because the company was still in its infancy, he asked for the state of Indiana. They gave it to him and little did they know that he would build it into an $8 billion-a-year business. And he stayed connected with everyone he did business with.

When I taught the idea of going into your favorite magazines and cutting out pictures of what you want, John went for it. He cut out pictures of people and houses he wanted and then put them in storage for four years. When he moved to California years later, I was in what he calls his vision room, his world mapping room. He had pulled everything out of storage and all of those pictures he had cut out four years ago were on a wall.

One wall had pictures of all the people John wanted to hang out with—and he did, every one of them. Each is a celebrated name, the who's who of the world. He also had a picture of his ideal home that he had cut out of *Architectural Digest.* When he had cut it out, he didn't know where the home was. He only knew it was on a hilltop overlooking a great expanse of water, and it had a triple-wide Olympic swimming pool. Now he's living there. When he bought it, he didn't even know that was the house he had viewed, mind-mapped, and story-boarded four years earlier because the board was in storage. Yet here it is, his home. John said, "We've got to get a picture of this." I was carrying my digital camera and someone there took a picture of us standing in front of his storyboard, four years later.

MEET THE GREATS

Can you meet all the greats in your field, in your energy orbit, in your place of discipline and expertise where you want to grow and glow? I think the answer is unequivocally, "Yes!" Write down all the names of people who will nourish your soul and nourish your possibilities into the future. I can't tell you how you're going to meet them, but write them down and operate on faith. Faith is the substance of things hoped for, the evidence of things not seen (Hebrews 11:1). All you have to do is decide to write down the names of who you are going to meet—and it will start to happen.

Maybe you can even put together a little photo album like the top salesman I met in Canada who carries around a little photo album of all the people he wants to meet. After he sells to someone, he shows the album and says, "Could you flip through here and see if you know anyone?" Usually the response is something like, "That's my brother-in-law." Or, "Yea, we bowl together." Or, "That's my cousin." Then the salesman says, "Would you mind calling him? I'd like to meet him."

You can meet with anyone if you really want to. Six degrees of separation is the idea that all people are six, or fewer, social connections away from each other. I think once you understand this, you're only one or two people away from anyone you want to meet. When you get it in your head, they will show up in your experience. I can't tell you how they're going to show up, I just promise you that they will.

For example, many years ago I wanted to meet Reverend Billy Graham, so I had a picture of him cut out and posted where I could see it. One day my wife and I were flying out of Orange County Airport and there was some sort of delay. The head of airport security was a woman my wife knew, so when we saw her we asked what the problem was. She said that Billy Graham was flying in. I told her I always wanted to meet him and asked if it was possible.

Dr. Graham got off the plane and it appeared to me that nobody recognized him. He was wearing a big hat, sunglasses, and had what looked like six or eight newspapers under his arm. Because I'd watched him, and I knew his gait and knew that was him. Then I saw about nineteen bodyguards quickly surround him. Nevertheless, I walked up to him, introduced myself, and we had a great half-hour discussion while he waited for his luggage.

Focus on expanding your volume of friendships and acquaintances. When you need something, you can use your network to get from where you are to where you want to be, with whomever you want. Shift your thinking from in terms of volume of relationships to specific connections that may at times include only one person who could be the mentoring relationship you need.

TUTELAGE

In all my research, I've never found one person who became super successful unless they had a great and inspiring mentor. It's amazing what can happen when you have the right mentor to help guide you. I was under the tutelage of Bucky Fuller. My friend Bob Allen was under the tutelage of Dr. Stephen Covey. I don't know anyone who becomes great unless they get with a mentor or friend, someone with whom they can coalesce and are like-minded.

When Earl Nightingale was running a small insurance company, he made a short but powerful tape and titled it *The Strangest Secret*. When his staff heard it, everybody wanted it. His mail and advertising was done by Lloyd Conant at the time, and Lloyd said he wanted to partner with Earl and help market the tape. Before long, they built the great Nightingale-Conant company—the world's leader in personal development and dedicated to helping people achieve happy and successful business and personal lives.

When you have that inner desire, your network of people will expand. I want you to have a sense and attitude of expectancy that you're going to cultivate a network that is irresistibly good, that you will find the mentor or mentors who will help you cultivate yourself to be the new, refined, enhanced, and improved you. You will enjoy huge benefits in life to make all your dreams come true.

My friend Dr. John Maxwell, the leadership guru of all leadership gurus, says at any given time we should have seven different mentors. When I was in graduate school, one of my professors said that the chairman emeritus of the design department was going to be speaking at the convention center on campus. He told me, "This man is one of the most eminent thinkers of all time. Let's walk over and listen to him." When we arrived, thousands of students were there to hear Dr. Buckminster Fuller. I don't know how I'd missed him, but I'd never even heard of him. We sat in the front row, and this guy just smiled and shone and wowed my soul.

Later that afternoon I applied for and got to be one of Bucky's research assistants, which also paid the rest of my way through graduate school. He touched my soul because he had bigger thinking going on. He talked about the "young world," which I felt part of, getting it together and making the world work for 100 percent of humanity. When I got up close and personal to Bucky, I learned that anyone who's become great has sometime during his or her career apprenticed with someone great for two or more years.

So what do you do to solicit a mentor? You ask what they need, what their short supply is, how you can source and serve them, and get for them what they want. For example, when we wanted the top publicist in the country, Ariel Ford, who was doing all the publicity for Dr. Deepak Chopra and Dr. Wayne Dyer and others, she wouldn't give me the time of day. So I called a psychiatrist friend with whom she worked and asked what Ford's shortfall was. He said her shortfall was time.

So I called her back and said, "Ariel, Bucky Fuller has taught me how to expand and contract time. Fuller only sleeps two hours a night, and his teacher, Albert Einstein, slept twelve hours a night. One is not more important or better than the other," I said. "If you'd like to know how to expand or contract time, you need to take me on as a client." She did. I wanted to mentor with the best of the best in publicity because marketing plus exposure in the book business equals sales, and that's what I wanted to have and make happen.

Mentors are useful to you because they push you to your limit. It's like today in physical health. A physical coach can get you to do all the pushups you need to do. My physical personal trainer says, "All the way up, all the way down, hold that position, etc." And after a few minutes I'm trembling, but I really feel strong and feel on purpose. Well, that's what a mentor does. They pull out the best in you. They coach you to be who you can be so you don't stop before accomplishing what you want to accomplish.

I want to make sure that you keep cultivating not only seasoned relationships, but young relationships as well. Build bridges with younger people who are going to inspire you to do things that you didn't even think you could do. One of the many "impossible" tasks I've set for myself is to reforest the planet with 18 billion trees. I want to include fruit trees so everyone can pull off apples, pears, kumquats, plums, fresh, organic, live fruit whenever they're hungry.

A 9-year-old felt my energy when he heard that task of mine and said, "I'm going to be your mentee!" He wrote a book that generated 150,000 trees being planted. It's amazing what you can do if you just set your vision and decide to do it.

In the original *Star Trek,* Spock always bid farewell to his cherished friends by saying, "Live long and prosper." In the context we've been discussing, live long doesn't mean just taking one breath after another. It means staying in circulation, because you have to circulate to percolate. You have to meet new people, find new friends, make new partners, stay connected at the depth of your being—and for sure prosperity will follow, because prosperity means to be in the flow. When you stay connected, you're *in* the flow, you will *be* the flow, and you'll *create* the flow.

Every journey starts with the first step. Your first step starts with your next connection and that next connection will get you to the next and the next. You can have a meaning-ful, purposeful, invigorating life that will titillate every fiber of your being.

In an advance, "Congratulations!"

CHAPTER 7

THE GREATEST WEALTH

To be truly healthy is the greatest wealth. This is always a good cliché to think about and meditate on—*my health is my greatest wealth.* Your real personal wealth, your health equity, is the equity of all equities. In the beginning of our career life, many give their whole health to gain wealth; but in the end, a lot of people pay their whole wealth to regain their health.

You have to make sure you live healthfully, think healthy, talk healthy, act healthy, believe in your health, work at being healthy, and hang out with healthy people. It's important to eat vital, live, organic nutritional food and take supplements to prevent illness. My position is that you have to invest in both your health and your wealth.

A self-actualizing person at the very top of Maslow's hierarchy is one who is wealthy, healthy, happy, loved, beloved, joyous, expectant about life, has a lot to do, and wants to contribute at a deep and profound level.

Consider repeating, "My health is my greatest wealth," when you rise up in the morning and before you go to sleep every night—lull yourself to sleep. Repeat it 400 times if you can't go to sleep. Saturate your mind with the idea that you're debt-free, stress-free, and set free. Tell yourself, "I'm healthy, happy, wise, loving, loved, and beloved." If you say and believe that again and again, pretty soon it becomes the truth. It permeates your beingness and you start to be healthy at a level that maybe you never thought you could be healthy.

As a society, we spend more on elder care now than childcare; it's a remarkable statistic. Two thirds of all the people who have ever lived past 65 are alive right now. And in the past one hundred years, there's been a revolution in the prevention and treatment of illness. There's been a paradigm shift in the way Americans think about health.

In this chapter we will look at *three areas of health-related behaviors.* We're also going to talk about an anti-aging breakthrough and see what the truth is about staying fit at any age, which may be a bit different from what you expect.

NUMBER ONE: EXERCISE IS IMPORTANT

We've become a fitness-conscious nation. Early in the morning, at lunchtime, and at the gym in the evening, there are people exercising. Whole industries have sprung up around the benefits of exercise—Nike, Bowflex, etc. Although we are fitness conscious now more than ever and many are more robustly fit than ever, there are people who are more sedentary than ever, as well.

We have to pay attention to our physical well-being. It goes beyond shoes and exercise equipment, even beyond fitness sports stores and health clubs. We have to translate it into, "What am I going to do to make myself better than I've ever been, to pass my personal best." For example, start with five pushups a day, then work up to ten, then fifteen. Work to exceed your personal best. I busted through my personal best this morning when I was exercising, so I know it can be done, and you can do it too.

You can do the same with your wealth. Maybe start saving a dollar a day. A dollar a day over sixty-six years adds up to $25,000 if you're hiding it under your mattress or in your Folgers can. But at 10 percent interest, it turns out to be more than $1 million. But at 20 percent, which there are a lot of ways to get that, those are millionaire-rate returns. On a consistent, persistent, insistent basis, in one human lifetime of sixty-six years, it adds up to a billion dollars.

We're talking about physical equity and financial equity. Are they very much different? No. We're appreciating the asset called *you*. We're exercising you financially, emotionally, spiritually, and mentally. Why not? You are reading this book to learn how to have your equity grow and glow. That's what lifelong learning is about.

You need to grow and expand into the person you are meant to be. You may wonder, is that a divine and spiritual concept? Absolutely. All of us have an ethereal body where you grow from the top down, inside out, and you expand to morph into who you can be. That's who we're talking about; exercising the soul of you and making this a soul goal that you become impenetrable to illness.

Some people say, "I don't get sick, it's not part of the mantra that I believe. I don't get an annual cold. I don't get sniffles. I don't get the flu." They're being honest. And that's the position I've had now for more than thirty years, because I started studying this type of thinking. Can you get there? Yes. But the problem may be that you have to take care of yourself at higher levels. More Americans are overweight than ever before, and being overweight translates statistically into a higher rate of illness.

Priorities

We all have all the time we need for whatever we want to do. Bucky Fuller said we all have twenty-four hours in a day. But you either expand or contract time with your mind. Every priority has an anti-priority. Maybe you have made exercise an anti-priority. But if you aren't where you want to be and don't really feel good about yourself, why not make exercise a priority. You don't have to be perfect, just healthy. Why not find a picture of when you were a bit more youthful and healthy. Then put it on the mirror and look at it until you take ownership of it again.

I read a profile article about a 73-year-old who had been a lifeguard on Long Island for more than fifty years. He described one of the clearest changes he's seen in beach-goers in one eloquent sentence, "The bathing suits have gotten smaller and the people have gotten fatter." Absolutely that's the way it is—but it doesn't have to stay that way.

Although more money is being spent on health and fitness, at the same time one of the most important markers of poor health is becoming more prevalent. Clearly it's a mistake to lead a sedentary life and lifestyle that leads to becoming unhealthy and overweight. What's the right alternative? The truth is it's not simple or as painful as pounding the pavement or sweating it out in the gym.

A study that focused on a remarkable number of people on the island of Okinawa who lived past the one-hundred-year mark revealed the power of lifestyle over genetics. Lifestyle accounts for two-thirds of life expectancy, only one-third is due to genetics. This is the whole thing about nurture and nature. Your *nature* is what you're given; your *nurture* is what you decide to do with your nature. Your nurture is your own consciousness, awareness, your own study and thinking.

Okinawans are very active but they're not out jogging, revealed the study. They enjoy walking, hiking, swimming, martial arts, Tai Chi, and gardening. If you've never been to a Tai Chi or martial arts class, try it. They also do karate and traditional dance similar to Tai Chi that gives them cardio-vascular fitness, strength, flexibility, more graceful movement, and better balance.

Exercise keeps you lean, fit, feeling good, and sweaty, which detoxes your body. Exercise also keeps you flexible and gives you a greater equilibrium that reduces risks of falling, which is the major cause of illness and death in older people. One of my heroes was George Burns. When asked, "How do you live to be so old?" he said, "Keep breathing."

Exercise is the most effective work to combine with plea-sure, with an emphasis on pleasure. You feel better when you feel good. The basic recommendation is you wake up your met-abolics in the morning; that's what I like to exercise. Others run or walk at lunchtime; they skip lunch and de-stress. And others go to the gym after work for an hour. Now when you come home be face to face and 100 percent with your family. Is that important? I think so.

I'm not saying to become obsessive; but exercise gives us inner endorphins that we can either use or lose. I want you to use yourself. Mary Kay of Mary Kay Cosmetics said when your life's over, you look back, and you will either say you wore out and rusted out or you used yourself full out. I want you to use yourself full out. So ask yourself, *What are the things I like to do and how can I do them in ways that will enhance my overall physical condition?*

Definitely monitor yourself and consult a physician before starting any exercise program. Make sure you are doing what's best for you. The better we know ourselves, the better and longer we can live.

Eliminate the things that aren't direct health benefits; balance them with the demands of being healthy. If you want to spend Sunday afternoon watching a baseball game on TV, feel free to do so and recognize the benefits and pleasures that it brings you. But try taking a brisk walk twice around the block before the game starts. This will not only benefit your health, it will reduce your guilt that you may feel about spending the afternoon sitting down.

If possible, instead of riding the elevator, walk up the stairs for exercise. One of my great, ageless friends climbs eighteen flights of stairs in a neighborhood hotel three times a week. Studies have shown a correlation between a low heart rate and longevity. My friend's heart rate has a resting rate of 48.

Choose the exercise of your heart's desire. I don't care what you do, but do something. Exercise is action; build up moderately, progressively, and keep at it. The key point is that almost anything is better than nothing. Take at least a short walk every day, if possible. Walk alone, with your dog, or with a buddy who appreciates the benefits of exercise.

In business and in exercise, when we're building equity we're on the leading edge, the cutting edge—we're doing our best to advance our healthy selves.

NUMBER TWO: FOOD AND DIET ARE IMPORTANT

There was an amazing study done in Finland some years ago that made a tremendous impression on everyone who heard about it. Two statistically matched groups of middle-aged men were asked to follow very different diets. The first group was carefully monitored by doctors to see that any unhealthy foods were eliminated. The men in the other group could eat whatever they wanted.

The usual Finnish diet is very unhealthy by most standards. Yet the health of the unsupervised group proved to be much stronger than that of the careful eaters, especially regarding heart attacks. What's the lesson in the study? Does it mean that diet is unimportant and we can all head to the closest fast-food drive-thru for lunch? No. But it may mean that we don't have to head for wheat germ either. Perhaps even more, we need to recognize the effects of stress and diet. If stress is increased by radically changing what we eat, maybe we're doing more harm than good.

When people overeat or eat unhealthy foods, there's a reason—usually an emotional, subconscious reason. There also may be some level of satisfaction or pleasure that comes with those kind of foods. Sometimes food is the greatest pleasure people have in their lives. And for some people, if the food is eliminated, it has to be replaced by something else. To get rid of a bad habit, it has to be instantaneously replaced with a good habit. Finding a replacement requires insight.

That's what this book is really all about. It's discovering and rediscovering your dreams and translating them into realities. It's about changing your perceptions of life to turn toward the directions you desire, deserve, and choose in favor of yourself.

Having said all that, there's no doubt that adding more fruits and vegetables to your diet can have enormous health benefits. Most say you need five fresh fruits and vegetables a day and I suggest they be organic. If there are insecticides, herbicides, or pesticides on the fruits and vegetables, it causes harm. I studied with the world's greatest physiologist, an anatomist, so I understand what goes on at a cellular level.

Dick Gregory, a college classmate of mine, wrote a good book with natural diet recipes titled *Cookin' with Mother Nature.* Something is always in season whether berries, oranges, corn, beans, or whatever. When I fell out of the sky and went bankrupt, as I was climbing back up, I told myself that someday I would grow all my own fresh fruits and organic vegetables. I'd use composted, living soil that's vitally healthy and alive. And the food would be delicious and so good that it would recharge my body at a cellular level and fortify my whole immune system.

That's the truth of me now. You may have never had a really fresh beet. You may have never enjoyed fresh beet and carrot juice that just came straight out of the ground, was washed, ground up, and you drank it. I can literally feel how healthy it is when I drink it. Some recommend drinking five glasses of juice a day; and if you eat or drink all the red vegetables that regrow your whole DNA and RNA system, it makes you ageless. That plus the green vegetables. We now know for a fact that all the greens are the antioxidants that rebuild cells. Research at the Rockefeller Center says that if a cell has enough oxygen, it will never die in a body.

That's why we may be able to live to be 120 or even 150. It's going to take some changes in the way we think and eat, but everyone can be happy, healthy campers. You have to decide in favor yourself. You have to put it in writing. Then you have to put it in action and decide to move forward a little bit at a time. In the United States and in the world in general, we're using too many petrochemicals in our agricultural land and the life force energy of the land is becoming devitalized. There's a soul force in humanity that we have to work on to keep our resources high and vital.

Just like we take care of the equity called our body, we have to take care of the equity called our earth, which nourishes the food we eat. We want to get the highest vitality food to get the most energy. Question: who's going to do better, somebody with high energy or low energy? If you want to have high energy, you have to put in the jet fuel. If you're putting in the best stuff and your body is in the best condition, you will be ready to take on every obstacle and realize your dreams.

I'm asking you to look at these health issues anew and see with a fresh set of eyes. My friend Brian Tracy says, "Do zero-base thinking." Start at zero and ask yourself, *If I really want to have exercise equity and diet equity, what must I do to really take care of myself so I am the person who wakes up feeling great every morning and ready to rock and roll into life with vim, vigor, vitality, and enthusiastic excitement? How can I become healthy, happy, tuned in, and turned on?* I hope by now that you know the answer—a healthy diet and exercise.

NUMBER THREE: EMOTIONAL HEALTH

The last health-related behavior area to discuss is emotional health. During the past several decades, there have been some revolutionary and evolutionary changes in the way people approach issues of emotional health, particularly those pertaining to people past the age of 40. Remember, we never had such a large group of people maturing and so many people thinking about it.

There has been the introduction of all kinds of antidepressant and antianxiety drugs that has transformed the way people view emotional problems. Those type of drugs are now advertised during TV sports events, right beside beer commercials. Many millions think that if they pop a pill, they can get well. A cure for a disease doesn't come out of a pill. Pills are good for treating symptoms, but they're not necessarily good for the ground-level cure.

There are many benefits to the pharmaceutical revolution—if considered with wisdom and insight. Understand that just like the "Father of Medicine" Hippocrates said, "Physician heal thyself," you are your own first line of defense. You are your own physician. Before you go to a physician, make sure the physician is intrinsically wise, trustworthy, and has your best interests at heart.

You have to understand that medicine nowadays is a business. If you go to a surgeon, the surgeon thinks of you with a knife in his or her hand. If you go to a chiropractor, he or she will see you as needing an adjustment. If you go to a consultant, you will be told that you need more consulting. I'm asking you to be a wise consumer of goods. If you need a physician, I want you to go to a credible and competent physician or a health-care person.

As throughout this book, I want to you to look anew, rethink, be of a new mind. Regarding emotional health, you may want to consider that it is more complex than you think. Maybe you could look in different places and in different ways for help. You have to keep expanding your aura of influence and the people you meet, because there are different solutions that you may not hear or you may not read unless you start looking at new possibilities. Some people don't even know they don't feel as good as they could feel.

It's a mistake to rely on medication for a solution of what Freud called the "problem of happiness." There's no reason why anyone should try to do so. For example, multiple studies have shown regular, vigorous exercise and laughter produce changes in the brain chemistry comparable to those of the best drugs, and you don't need a prescription.

Sleep Deprivation

And there are many other well-documented ways to optimize emotional health including getting enough sleep. I want to talk a little bit about sleep deprivation because 60 million Americans are purportedly sleep deprived. I was sleep-deprived for a while; I was having dizzy spells and passing out. I asked the doctor I was running with in Florida, and he said, "Tell me about your sleep cycle. Do you wake up to an alarm clock every day?"

I said, "Yes."

He said, "Then you're sleep deprived." And I immediately got it.

As you read earlier, my teacher, Bucky Fuller, slept only two hours every night. And his teacher, Albert Einstein, slept twelve hours. One is not necessarily better than the other. Fuller said that when you're going to go into your sleep cycle, you have to say, "I'm going into REM (Rapid Eye Movement) sleep and wake up two hours from now refreshed." You need at least one 90-minute cycle a night when you dream. That's when you see someone's eyes twitch underneath their eyelids. That's REM sleep.

Americans worry about school, work, family, health issues, or whatever, and we wake up. You need to be telling yourself, *I'm going into REM sleep, and when I wake up* (how many hours), *I'm going to wake up refreshed.* And when you do, you're going to feel really good. Next, avoid negative stimulation that is constantly delivered to us via various media. I saw an example of that when I came back from college one time. My mother had thirteen locks on our kitchen door.

"Why are there thirteen locks on the door?" I asked her.

She said, "In Chicago an old lady my age got raped."

"That's an hour and a half away from here." But she listens to the news on the radio all day long while she irons, washes clothes, makes a meal, and then she watches the news with my dad at 6 o'clock.

There are two basic ways we learn—one is impact and the other is repetition. If we repeat garbage into our heads on a full-time basis, we'll live in fear, anger, doubt, indecision, pain, procrastination, and guilt. Avoid negative stimulation.

I watch things that are uplifting, stimulating and life-enhancing rather than watching the news again and again and again. That's why I love audio books, because they make your drive time, learn time. The recordings make your car a little classroom on wheels. Even when I exercise, I never go out and run with my dogs without wearing a headset.

Increasing Your Emotional Quotient

How do you increase your emotional quotient? Laughter is one way! Dr. Norman Cousins was my teacher, and twenty years ago he was told, "You're going to die, pal, you have too much stress. You need to just lay here in the hospital and quietly let it go." He had been following a McGill University study proving that laughter stimulates 134 positive healing chemistries in the mind; like endorphins, they are natural interrupters that go on red alert and start to heal the body. So Cousins, a self-determining man, said, "I'm outta here!" He checked himself out of the hospital and checked into a hotel room. He watched every funny movie he could find—and he laughed.

The one that caused the greatest blood serology change for him was watching Alan Funt when he went to the border between New Jersey and Pennsylvania, and at 5 o'clock in the morning, he put up a sign that read: "Pennsylvania CLOSED." Cars were lined up along the road with drivers asking when it would reopen. Well, Cousins roared with laughter—and he recovered in weeks. Cousins lived twenty years longer than any medical professional had predicted he could possibly live. His healing was so miraculous, unique, and unusual that he wrote an instant best seller, which I encourage you to read or listen to—its title is *Anatomy of an Illness.*

Many others had similar health and healing breakthroughs. Dr. Cousins was a PhD, not a medical doctor, but nonetheless he was invited to be on the faculty at UCLA Medical School. To his absolute amazement and utter astonishment, he discovered that medical students only studied disease and sickness, never prevention.

Cousins decided to laugh his way well. I hope you saw the movie *Patch Adams* starring by Robin Williams. Based on a true story, Dr. Patch Adams realized that people got well if they knew somebody cared about them personally. People got well if they had fun. He treated kids with debilitating diseases by going into hospital rooms dressed in a clown outfit and being silly.

Dr. Adams found that humor naturally alleviates pain, and in some cases could heal chronically ill people—especially children. We need more laughter, joy, happiness, and exuberance in our lives. We have to feel like we're champagne bubbles bubbling up and overflowing with joy. "I'm having fun having fun"—visualize that. Use that as one of your thought affirmations and mantras. An affirmation is something you say to yourself, say to others, and say it enough times that you believe it, think about it, act upon it—and then it acts upon you.

You need to be systematically programming yourself to have happy, joyous experiences. Listen to funny stuff and people who make you laugh. Purposely push some humor and laughter and high spirits into your workday. All people have their emotional butterfly stepped on occasionally, so we have to keep instigators of lightheartedness near us. We need endorphins gushing in our body. Humor is vital for our emotional health. When you're feeling blue or down, use laughter to get your emotional metaphorical butterfly to go into high flight again.

Your mind can only think one thought at a time; it can think a lot of thoughts in sequence, but basically just one thought at a time. Humor, like music, is so powerful and pervasive as a tool that it will help you conquer fear, alleviate adversity, regenerate your spirit, and get those inner endorphins and positive chemistries rocking and rolling inside your body. Humor will help you soar to new heights.

We're fortunate to live in a time and a place where a human being no longer has to be totally discouraged. You can create and maintain health in the best of all possible ways with exercise, good nutrition and diet, and with a good emotional attitude. You can start hanging out with people who are emotionally nourishing to you—people who are positive and always see more in you than you see in yourself.

And sooner than later, you will be resolutely healthy; your immune system's going to be strong. You're going to be happy, fit, and totally on top of your world. You're going to have more energy than you've ever had before.

So on behalf of all that kind of activity, I congratulate you in advance.

CHAPTER 8

SPIRITUAL EXPERIENCES

For more than 400 years, since the time of Isaac Newton, Western society has understood the universe in terms of a mechanical model. The universe is like a finely balanced machine governed by physical forces that are complex but understandable in their day-to-day operation. Gravity, for example, is a force that causes the apple to fall to the ground from the tree rather than taking off into space. Gravity is also the force that keeps the planets balanced in their orbits around the sun. We may not know exactly what gravity is, but at least we know how it works.

There are a few problems with a mechanical model of reality, however. Some may seem merely philosophical at first, but they add up to the need for taking another look at what's really going on in the world around us—and in our own hearts and minds as well.

Since the revolutionary discoveries of Albert Einstein, science no longer believes that the universe is anything like a machine. Rather, it's like an endlessly expanding piece of rubber, perhaps an alphabet, or even a thought in the mind of

God. But it's not like a car parked in your driveway; rather, everything is in motion.

It's interesting that the man often credited, or blamed depending how you look at it, for the creation of the mechanistic view of the universe is Sir Isaac Newton. He was secretly one of the great mystical thinkers of his time. Newton actually spent more time studying alchemy than classical physics. He was also a deeply religious man. What does that tell us about the founder of modern science—one of the greatest thinkers who ever lived? His was a profoundly spiritual view of world.

What does it tell us when Albert Einstein makes the statement, "God does not play dice with the universe"? What does it tell us when a book entitled *The Physics of Immortality* is written by a world-class physicist named Frank J. Tipler— with a thesis that all human beings will be resurrected at the end of time, and the thesis is backed up with thirty pages of scientific notes?

At the very least, I believe this tells us there's something in a human heart, mind, and soul and perhaps especially in the educated, intelligent heart, mind, and soul that yearns for an explanation of the world beyond the level of changing the tire on a car. I've noticed this yearning seems to take hold more strongly as we become more mature in years. As Mark Twain said, "If you believe in God when you're 20, you probably don't have a brain. If you don't believe in God at 60, you probably don't have a heart." Also, having been in three war zones with active fighting, I can assure you that no military person goes into a foxhole without God.

I remember when I was in Vietnam, I could tell the difference between incoming and outgoing bombs—and I was very good at moving underneath a bed in a nanosecond. I have to believe the God Twain spoke of was not necessarily the old man with a beard sitting on a cloud. I think what Twain meant by God was simply the presence of a Power beyond the limits of our rational understanding. God is the Cause that causes, the Intelligence behind all intelligence.

FIVE SPIRITUAL EXPERIENCES IN LIFE

I can think of at least five areas in life where the belief in a concept of God or spiritual power becomes more important as we get older. In each of these five areas, this belief enhances our desire, perhaps our ability, to realize our dreams. I hope you've had a chance to connect with these areas of spiritual experience; but if you haven't, it's never too late. Let's examine each.

The experience of parenthood is a deeply spiritual component of life. Being a parent is a much more all-inclusive concept than it was even a few decades in the past. Today there are two-parent families, one-parent families, adoptive families, single sex families, all possible combinations. We no longer just have the Hallmark image of a type of family or what is seen on television shows like *Ozzie and Harriet* and *Leave it to Beaver.*

It is my opinion that one thing is true of all forms of parenthood, you don't make this journey without glimpsing something beyond a purely mechanical view of life. For example, I gave the birthing bath to each of my adopted daughters. Allow me to share that as I gently cleansed Elizabeth, our two hearts literally joined as one. To my eyes, it was symbolically a rainbow that connected our two hearts. I could feel her heart energy, called an India heart chakra, and she could feel mine. That is a miracle that is totally, absolutely unforgettable.

The second area is the *experience of time.* As we get older, time not only seems to go faster but it actually does go faster because time does not exist separately from our perception of it. As Albert Einstein said, "Time goes slower when you're sitting on a hot stove than when you're sitting on a park bench holding your girlfriend's hand." That's called the Theory of Relativity. Time is a perceived duration, and a perception speeds up. I think there's a spiritual message to be found in this experience. How can we make the most of the time that's given to us?

I want to expand our experience of whether time goes fast or slow. I want to suggest that you make this one of your mastermind family table conversations, and a conversation to have with your best friends.

I learned this positioning from my writing partner, Bob Allen. He asks questions about absolutely everything and then lets the audience respond. So as I was writing about this, one night we were sitting at our dinner table with some guests and our kids, and I said to the teenagers, "When does time go slowly and when does time go quickly?" The teenager who is a freshman in high school said, "Time goes slow when you're taking a bad test or when you're dreading a test or when you're excited about the big party, but you don't go."

Our 16-year-old said, "Time goes slow your whole 15th year when you're waiting to get a driver's license." Uncle Jimmy said, "Time goes slow when you're 20 and you want to be 21 so you can drink." Time goes slowly when you're bored and you're not in control and you've lost a sense of yourself.

But time goes quickly when you're totally and absolutely focused, when you're turned on, and when you have a great and inspiring teacher or project. Time goes fast during a test and you know you're going to do well. Time goes fast when you're the in zone, whether playing tennis or performing on stage—that's being the best we can be.

Wayne Dyer told me that one time he was suddenly stuck at his place for six hours—he couldn't leave. There was a pair of ice skates there, and he put them on. Although he hadn't skated in thirty years, in a few seconds he was back in the zone of being a great ice skater again. He used to play hockey as a kid.

Time goes fast when you're going someplace enjoyable and exciting. When is the last time you have gone into a time warp?

Wayne Dyer and I were speaking on a radio show one time and the journalist said to Dr. Dyer, "You say you can fly." Wayne said, "Yeah. I fly all the time in my dreams." Time warp happens in our dream state. And when you bring a dream state into your life, dreams come true. You can make deposits of time in your head. I'm asking you to explore this whole concept of time. Figure out when time goes fast and slow for you.

We have only one shot in this bag of skin and behind this set of eyeballs. We have 10, 20, to 100 times more life experiences than our grandparents or great-grandparents ever had. Avoid wasting time—use it to your advantage.

The experience of nature makes me think of a trip to Death Valley, California. If you go there, drive up to the top of one of the peaks and overlook the valley. There's a little sign there that describes what you're seeing and where you're seeing it from. It says the rocks you're standing on at that point are over a billion years old. It's very hard to wrap our minds around the idea of a billion years, and it's certainly a different perspective than we use every day—a genuinely spiritual perspective. When we reflect on the forces that are much bigger, more powerful, and more lasting than we are, we step into a spiritual experience of nature.

I took my dad to the Grand Canyon and we marveled at the vastness. We need to find a place and space where we're best in contact with nature and feel our intrinsic spiritual home. For some it's forests in the mountains while hiking, biking, or skiing. When I'm on top of Big Bear or any of the great mountains I like to ski on, the vistas are amazing. I breathe in fresh, clean air and have pristine scenes of pine trees, crisp white snow, and Big Bear Lake at the bottom. It is enchanting. For others, beaches are where they feel most connected to nature. I love the beaches, too.

Other people connect with the desert and the scenery and environment there. In Arizona there are extraordinary, extravagant, and lavishly beautiful landscapes. If you've never been to Tucson, it's worth the trip to go through the museum and see the thousands of different kinds of plants and structures and cacti. There are a thousand different kinds of aloe vera plants. When you branch out to different areas of the country, you gain respect for the variety in our world.

I connect best on the Big Island of Hawaii; as far as I'm concerned it's a Mecca center. It attracts spiritually awake, alive, enthusiastic, tuned in, turned on people. It has eleven of the thirteen climate zones. It is the biggest of the islands in the Hawaiian chain. Half of the Big Island is desert, the Kona side. It has to be irrigated to bloom, which is just like Southern California. But when it's irrigated, it is absolutely, completely gorgeous when landscaped. The other half of the Big Island is the rainforest where all kinds of flora and fauna grow. It's so much fun there because in the middle of winter you can get dropped on top of Mauna Kea and ski down. You have to heli-ski; but you can ski down seven miles—in a swimming suit. So it's got everything.

Number four is the *experience of coincidence,* or more precisely "synchronicity." In everyone's life there are times when things seem to happen that completely contradict the laws of probability. As we get older, truly incredible coincidences begin to become more and more apparent—and we wonder what could be behind the incidents.

Arthur Koestler wrote a wonderful book titled *The Roots of Coincidence.* It asserts that coincidence is actually a quick glimpse into the spiritual world, a reminder that we should be paying attention to spiritual forces that are at work every moment of our life. Every time you get in any transportation vehicle, whether a bus, plane, or train, say to yourself, *I'm going to sit next to and meet the person who is going to take me to the next level on my life's journey.*

I've been telling you throughout this book that dreams don't have deadlines. It's true. Your imagination creates your reality; whatever you think about, comes about. Your imagination is going to create coincidences because your intention in that tension will get you retention of your dreams.

And the fifth is the *experience of realization that life will have an end.* Death is an inevitable reality. We shouldn't shy away from this crucial aspect of life. The writer William Saroyan's last words were, "Everybody has to die, but I have always believed an exception would be made my case." I think all of us sort of feel that way. I've taught that you need to keep a positive mental attitude, because actually there are no exceptions. We may use the knowledge that life has an end to better understand and appreciate life while we're living it.

The inevitability of physical death, however, raises a question of whether there are other ways of living beside our physical bodies. In fact, I believe there are many ways. The ancient Chinese believed no one was dead as long as there was someone who remembered them. Vikings had the same belief. We can live on through works of art, journals, writings, collections of photographs, pictures, videos, and some people opt to be remembered through foundations dedicated to helping others.

Andrew Carnegie is immortalized through his philanthropic endeavors. His legacy includes building more than 1,600 libraries in the United States and 2,500 worldwide. His fortune supported the discovery of insulin, and he was dedicated to principles of scientific philanthropy and promoting education and international peace. Carnegie said, "To try to make the world in some way better than you found it is to have a noble motive in life."

The other way you can live and keep living is through organ donorship. It is my position that when you die, the best thing to do is give away your organs to those in need. I'm an organ donor—I think it's the right thing to do. I understand this may be a controversial position. You may have a spiritual belief system that doesn't allow it. Maybe it is something that violates your sensibilities. Remember, I want you to think some new thoughts, one may be to perpetuate yourself through organ donorship. When you're done with your eyes, why not let somebody else have them?

There is a classic story in *Chicken Soup for the Soul 2* about a woman who was told by her doctor she didn't have long to live. She decided to contribute all her body parts. She was a schoolteacher and there were some things she wanted to do before the end.

It's that age-old question—if you knew you only had six months to live, what would you do? If you knew unequivocally that you were going to have a stroke or heart attack and were going to leave your physical form and go back to pure spirit, what would you do?

The woman said she always wanted to create artwork; she really had a talent. And she wanted to keep teaching because she loved the kids. She also wanted to write poetry. Well, she did all those things; and her poetry was published, and her artwork sold for a high amount.

She had decided to give away her organs; her eyes went to a recipient in the Carolinas. The man was so profoundly touched, as he had been blind his whole life and suddenly could see. He went to the eye bank and said, "I know it's out of protocol and that the highest giving is anonymous giving, but I would like to meet and thank the parents of the donor." The person at the eye bank had a soft, compassionate heart and said yes and told the man where the parents lived. He flew to Staten Island on Saturday morning and showed up unannounced.

The mother of the donor opened the door and he told her the story and thanked her. She said, "Young man, you have to spend the weekend with us," which he did. Sunday night before he was about to leave and fly home, the mother said to him, "When I look at you, I see somebody I know. Do you mind if I run upstairs and get the last picture that Linda ever painted? It's a picture of her ideal man." She brought it downstairs and the painting had verisimilitude, exact similarity to this young man. And the last poem she wrote was: "Two hearts in the night, two hearts falling in love and passing in the night, never able to gain each other's sight." Maybe they were soulmates and never met each other.

I mentioned that story when speaking at a major church in Detroit. Afterward when I was signing books for about 400 people, twin brothers came up to me. One looked healthy and the other looked like he had jaundice. I get goose bumps as I tell you this *Chicken Soup* experience I had. The one brother said, "I need an organ transplant and the only person who is compatible is my twin brother. And until he heard the story you just told about Linda, he'd never share it with me."

In an interview that was done shortly before the great author and adventurer Ernest Hemingway died, the journalist asked, "Why do you stand at an architect-slanted table and keep writing day after day when you're wracked with the pain of arthritis and a failing body? My gosh, man, you've written best-selling books, you've won a Pulitzer Prize, you've been everywhere, met everyone, done everything."

Hemingway responded, "Because I still have stories to tell. People still want to read and watch my stories on the big screen—the pain passes, but the stories last."

Like Hemingway, your story is yours to create, master, share, constantly reinvent, recount, and then later on to be remembered and to last in history. You are here to make a significant spiritual difference now and forever. Because *the spiritual you is eternal.*

SPIRITUAL WHOLENESS

Let's talk about 360 degrees of spiritual wholeness. If you're filling up this sphere, are you at 10 percent of who you could be? Are you at 50 percent? Have you really done your spiritual work in whatever it is? Do you know how you can approach 100 percent? In a spiritual realm to get to 100 percent, it seems to me that you need to get a bounce off somebody who is a spiritual leader to you. You also have to have somebody you consider spiritual so you can ask questions and discuss spiritual matters.

You are a spiritual voyager, a spiritual journalist in your own quest to understand who you are and who is God during this lifetime. This is something to journal about—and do it independently. It's nice to get the answers at our church, temple, synagogue, ashram, or mosque, but at some point you have to get weaned and ask yourself when you're journaling: *What do I believe? Who do I believe in? How do those beliefs become actionable in my life? What am I going to do about them?*

These are big questions and big issues. But you have a big life—or you wouldn't be reading *Dreams Don't Have Deadlines.* You are bigger than you think you are. You're more spiritual than you think you are, and you probably have a role that is much bigger than you've led up to now.

William Shakespeare said that all life is a stage—and the whole stage of life has a spiritual basis. Teihard de Chardin, one of the great Catholic mystics, said we're spiritual beings in a spiritual universe. Many think we're just physical beings in a spiritual universe; but if we're spiritual beings in a spiritual universe, then we have a spiritual activity to be about.

The question you have to ask yourself, *What activity am I supposed to be about?* In Christian literature, it says you're supposed to be about your Father's business, and your Father's business is something to figure out what it means to you— because it's one of the dreams that you're here to manifest.

CHAPTER 9

GENEROSITY

An ancient fable that has passed through many cultures concerns a man who is given the privilege of visiting both Heaven and hell and discovering the difference between the two.

First, his guiding angel took him to hell. There he saw a group of people seated around large tables covered with the most delicious food, yet all the people seemed to be starving to death. They were as thin as skeletons. The reason for their condition was very clear. Although spoons were chained to their hands, the handles were too long for them to put any food into their mouths. So despite the wonderful food, no one got anything to eat.

The man said, "Wow, that looks pretty bad. Let's see what Heaven looks like." He was shown another room that was exactly the same as the first. Once again there was a table stacked with food and a group of people seated around the table with long spoons chained to their hands. But these people were extremely happy and certainly well-fed. Again, the reason was clear and simple. Instead of trying to feed themselves, they were feeding each other.

Sharing is having more. The best way to get something, is to give something. I see this time as the greatest, most inspiring giving time in history.

EIGHT LAWS OF GIVING

I've created what I call the *eight laws of giving;* and remember, giving is really the flip side of getting—helping people achieve their dreams is inseparable from achieving your own. Keep that in mind as we explore these principles in this chapter.

Giving Principle One

When you give, you receive. God is the greatest Giver. God's nature is to give. In God's giving, He teaches us to give. Be generous and come from abundance. God can never run out of anything because He made it all. Only God knows how to really give. God's giving perpetually creates more. God's giving never stops, and God never stops giving. God is a relentless Giver. He gives and gives. God's giving does not hurt. God's giving only makes God more—God's giving never makes God any less. God's giving is great, continuous, and inexhaustible. God's giving is an everlasting multiplication of all supply. God is perpetually modeling how we are to individually and collectively give and keep giving.

Everyone knows that one times zero is zero. Anything times zero is zero. However, one times God is infinite. Even if you have low self-esteem and don't feel like a whole person temporarily, *you times God is infinite,* so use infinity to multiply yourself. Make yourself a masterpiece. Become more of who you really are. One times the infinite has to be infinite, and you are the one, the only one who can choose to multiply yourself times God. God is ready when you are; therefore, you times God is infinite. Each of us times God is infinite.

When you and God unify, you become one with God. Only you can become an individualization of God. Like giving in human form, you start to multiply the infinite. It's miraculous. God needs each of us to multiply all of us. God needs each of us to multiply out all that's possible for the rest of us. You are more important than you have ever realized.

It's only when we shut off giving that we create lack. A lack of consciousness creates lack in our experiences in life. Start all your thinking with giving, and you will experience perpetual happiness, plenty, abundance, and loads of surplus. The ultimate in godliness is giving; the more we give, the closer we are to God—we become more connected to the Source when we give.

My friend Cynthia Kersy, author of the best-selling book *Unstoppable,* says it's impossible to understand giving from a human point of view—except by experience and after the fact. It happens mystically and mysteriously; every time you give, you get. Ultimately and inevitably you get from somewhere, somehow, and at some time. Be godlike; be a great giver.

The only way to interrupt your supply is to stop giving. Only you can stop the flow. You alone have the power to turn on your giving spigot or turn off your giving spigot. You alone can turn it. The Infinite doesn't care because it's infinite. The Infinite is neutral and shows no favoritism. There's no more life in an ant than an elephant.

Wise giving or having a lot or a little is *your* decision. Once you know, love, spiritually respect yourself and use this awareness, you become unstoppable. The original translation in the Bible says that God loves a hilarious giver (2 Corinthians 9:7). The words were downplayed to "cheerful giver," meaning laugh, enjoy yourself knowing in your heart of hearts that there is more and better coming.

The Infinite has all there is. Jesus said it is your Father's good pleasure to give you the Kingdom (Luke 12:32). The Kingdom is yours and mine for the asking. The Kingdom includes the resources that are literally inexhaustible, the invisible resources are totally inexhaustible—and the visible resources that come out of the invisible resources are practically inexhaustible.

When psychiatrist Victor Franco was in a Nazi concentration camp, he traded the one pea he was given daily for food to other prisoners for their allotment of water. That trade of food and his deep, deep desire to see his beloved wife one more time to say, "I love you," is what kept him alive. Trading a pea for water kept him alive until he saw her again and was everlastingly reunited.

Giving Principle Two

We are made in the image and likeness of God. If we're God's greatest and highest reflection, then we too are to be great. Jesus said the greatest among you is a servant of all (Matthew 23:11). Our greatness is available only through service and giving to others. Your soul is here to serve and serve greatly. Your objective is to find a place where you can and want to serve in a spirit of absolute joy. Discover a way to utilize your extraordinary talent so you can experience it as effortless effort.

As mentioned previously, Cavett Robert said that service is the rent we pay for the space that we occupy. Why not entertain the idea that you can be a colossal server-giver? Colossal giving and serving always guarantees colossal receiving. We are God stuff and good stuff. God and good are only one zero different. The zero can make you a hero if you think from God's point of view.

In your early morning prayers and meditations, take God into your heart. Use His mind to think through what you should be doing. As you really get quiet and are praising and raising God in your mind, you'll have distracting thoughts that may be God's ideas or answers for your future, your good, and/or your greatness. God talks to us only when we're quiet enough to listen and hear, when there are no distractions of business, phones, kids, noise, and interruptions. God has bountiful messages for each of us.

Dr. George Washington Carver was born in a time of slavery. In 1865, he witnessed his mother being carried off as a slave when he was only 4 years old. Fortunately he was orphaned to parents who helped him learn to read. Carver was the first black man to graduate with a PhD in agriculture from Iowa State. Booker T. Washington appealed to his sense of justice and humbly requested Dr. Carver to come and teach "his people," meaning the black Americans at Tuskegee University. When Carver arrived, he saw that the cotton fields in the south were overexploited and the boll weevil was destroying all that was left.

While in the fields, Dr. Carver started talking out loud to God every morning at 4 o'clock, asking for providential help. Carver heard God tell his soul and spirit to grow legumes to put nitrogen back into the soil, as those plants absorb it straight from the air and put it back into the soil. It worked— soybeans and peanuts flourished. Carver had taken practically nothing and turned it into something great and profitable, and re-fertilized the soil simultaneously.

Eventually, though, the farmers were overproducing peanuts. They came to Dr. Carver with the problem. Carver again went into deep prayer and meditation at 4 a.m. asking for a solution. Consequently, he invented 362 uses for the peanut, including peanut butter, and rescued the beleaguered farmers from the overproduction.

Any one of us can take nothing and turn it into something with right thinking and right spirituality. God has special task assignments and obligations that only you can fulfill. Just like only I could have written this to you. I wrote it when I was coming out of a quiet meditation time and prayerful time on an airplane. I could hear God telling me that you're going to read this, understand it, and immediately put it into wonderful practice.

My friend Dr. Ken Blanchard said to me once, "When you wake up, wake up slowly." I interpreted that to mean to have a conversation with God before racing busily into the day's activity. God has ways of making your life operate with effortless ease and effort. If you just get quiet, be patient, and reverently listen, the more and better you get at it, the more God will tell you.

Perhaps you need to get up ten minutes earlier in the morning so you can "Be still" (Psalm 46:10) and ask God to talk to you. God will talk if you'll listen, pay attention, and then work to execute His plans. God has great plans for you (Jeremiah 29:11). Nelson Mandela prayed to God for extended stretches during his twenty-seven years in prison. Upon gaining freedom, he became South Africa's most beloved, revered, and respected president of all time.

How we treat each other is important to God. Why? Because He values us. He says He counts every hair on our head (Luke 12:7). Your self-esteem is important; as it's enhanced and increased, your value goes up. Jesus said, "Love your neighbor as yourself" (Matthew 22:39). The more positively and correctly we love ourselves, grow, improve, get stronger, have more wisdom, and become deeper in our character and our persona, the more and better we can source and serve and inspire our neighbors to do so as well.

One of the richest men in Australia, my friend Peter J. Daniels, author of *How to Be Happy though Rich,* says you can never be greedy as long as you're a tither who tithes. Likewise I say, you can never be greedy as long as you're a giver who gives. When you start to give all the time, a variety of different, worthwhile, and important things will start to happen in your life. Research proves that when people are asked to give, they give more if they're givers. Conversely, people who don't get asked, don't give at all.

Tithing means to give back 10 percent of essentially all that you receive. I believe tithing is an umbrella protection that can only help you if you've given in advance. If you choose to be a giver—giving away your time, talent, resources, smiles, connections, ideas, stuff, friendship, and your fun—good blessings will keep flowing back to you in ways known and unknown.

I encourage you to start by giving away your ideas, and more will come to you than you ever experienced before.

Giving Principle Three

Give yourself as part of the gift. The best giving always includes *you* as part of the gift. When you participate in a gift, its value is always more cherished and appreciated. When you give your presence and your essence, the gift's worth is infinitely more. When your soul and heart are part of the gift, the gift is permanently treasured and never forgotten. You actively make the gift into a successful outcome in advance.

Donors love to give to causes that fit their needs, wants, and desires. They want to give back and make the blind child see, or whatever is important to them. It converts one value into another—money into results in a field. Money can go many places that you cannot, and can do it all at the same time. I once heard W. Clement Stone say, "I got rich so my money could go out and source and serve people in places everywhere around the world." I thought that was such a charitable idea! If you have enough money to contribute, you can be multiplied in places doing great things and great work simultaneously.

Each of us is mightily blessed. We all have lots and lots to give, especially when you think creatively about giving. You can be a gift and a giver to someone, somehow, sometimes, somewhere—if you decide to be. People say, "I have nothing to give." That's not true. You can always give your smile, sincerity,

appreciation, humor, compassion, thankfulness, hugs, friendship, advice, a pat on the back, direction, example, and your
thinking. You can't be lonely if you positively and correctly
give yourself away.

I humbly ask you to do the height of giving and serving
greatly without expectation of return by giving the gift of your
organs and tissue upon your death. When you say I have nothing, you deny yourself. In truth, you have an abundance of
nonmaterial things to give; and when you give them, they open
up vast amounts of material things for you to give. It takes the
intangibles to make the tangibles. It takes nonmaterial gifts
to make material gifts. Decide that in truth you are generous.

Bob Allen says the decisions you make with each and every
dollar under your dominion determines whether you are on
course to become a millionaire or a pauper. How do you give
when you're poor? You're only poor if you're poor in consciousness. If you're poor in consciousness, you're poor in spirit. Why
not decide to be a giver.

We have a story in *Chicken Soup for the Soul* where a minister is looking out among the congregation and says, "We
have one family here that's in desperate need. They've got tat-
tered clothes. They don't have enough food to eat. They don't
have a car. I hope the whole congregation will give to this
congregant family."

The minister is in his study the next day, and the poorest
family, the one he was trying to aggregate goods for, comes
into the office pulling a little wagon behind them with all
kinds of fruit and wrapped-up, worn-out clothes. They said,
"We'd like to give and help those people you talked about

yesterday." The pastor's eyes filled and overflowed with tears because these were the people he was trying to help. Yet they were willing to give and help somebody they thought was less well-off than they were.

Giving Principle Four

Choosing to give is the first step to giving. I heard my friend Paul J. Meyer say that he wanted to give away a billion dollars during his lifetime. It inspired me to write it down as a goal. Perhaps hearing about something like that will inspire you to write down that as your goal. Or at least expand your desire to give faithfully. You may want to consider giving away your goods while you're still alive and can enjoy the fruits of your giving. In death, deep pockets are useless—and giving cannot be well-controlled from the grave.

Two examples: The Bishop Estate in Hawaii was dedicated to educating every native-born person in Hawaii. The bountiful financial resources of the estate would have done just that. Unfortunately, a corrupt board of directors decided to overpay themselves and took outrageous salaries of $1,800,000 each. They violated the intentions of the trust and were sent to prison.

Another example is the John Paul Getty Museum. John Paul Getty was exceedingly frugal during his life. He made a vast fortune predominately in the oil business and buying stock during the bottom of the Depression. He invested $30 million in undervalued stock. Everyone told him he was going to lose his shirt and go bankrupt. But his fortune kept growing and growing. He became the best collector of Greco Roman art and artifacts in the world and put them all in a museum in Malibu, California. When he died, he dedicated his money to the biggest and best museum in the world, which became the Getty Center outside LA, which is now free to the public. Richard Meier, world-famous architect, built the most exquisite museum.

But you can't control your money from the grave. I read in *The LA Times* that the directors of the museum bought themselves Rolls-Royces. Although I never met John Paul Getty, who was the richest man in the world while he was alive, I can guarantee you that he would be furious at such a misuse of his estate money, which had grown to $4 billion, making it the richest museum in the world.

If you're going to give your money away, maybe you can set up a foundation that's incorruptible. But if you don't think you can do that, why not give it away while you're alive. Set up a foundation so it grows and give it the best guidance and the best direction you can so your benefactions can be witnessed and the results enjoyed, hopefully while you're still alive. It's what you become in the process earning the money that makes you more of whom you really are. The process will wake you up to new levels of creativity, experience, and possibility.

The poster boy for giving is Paul Newman. He made $20 million per movie, and he created Newman's Own to go on into perpetuity. Oprah Winfrey has always been a tither, giving 10 percent of her earnings. When I received my seventh honorary doctorate at the University of Toledo, they asked me to give a presentation, at which we raised $100,000 and they dedicated it to a scholarship for business excellence in my name. I thought, *One hundred thousand is not adequate. I'd like to ensure that this goes into perpetuity and runs on automatic.* So I asked Art Linkletter and others to speak, and we raised millions of dollars.

The formula is to give out of your own largesse, which I recommend and encourage, but I also recommend that you create some resource system of ongoing, automatic, axiomatic, self-perpetuating charity philanthropy to source and serve the causes and push back the frontier on what you believe in.

Bucky Fuller said sharing is having more; and when our orientation is others-oriented, we share and become more purposeful and better stewards of our resources, be they financial, talent, personal connections, or whatever. To achieve your dreams, you have to understand that dreams don't have deadlines, and givers give.

The following story courageously teaches leadership and what I've been sharing with you. My friend Dan Clark from Salt Lake wrote this story for one of our *Chicken Soup* books and is titled, "A Brother Like That."

> A friend of mine named Paul received an automobile from his brother as a Christmas present. On Christmas Eve, Paul came out of his office and a street urchin was walking around the shiny new car admiring it. He asked Paul, "Is this your car?"
>
> Paul nodded. "Yes, my brother gave it to me for Christmas."
>
> The boy was astounded. "You mean your brother gave it to you and it didn't cost you nothin'?"

Paul nodded again.

The boy said, "Wow, I wish…"

Of course Paul knew what the boy was going to wish for—a brother like that. But what the boy said next jarred Paul down to his heels.

"…I wish I could be a brother like that!"

Paul looked at the boy in astonishment then impulsively said, "Would you like to take a ride in it?"

"Yes, I'd love to do that!"

After a short ride, the boy turned toward the man with his eyes aglow and said, "Mister, would you mind driving in front of my house?"

Paul smiled. He thought he knew what the lad wanted, to show his neighbors what it could be like to ride in a big, new automobile. But Paul was wrong again.

"Will you stop here at those two steps?" the boy asked. He got out and ran up the steps. In a little while Paul heard him coming back down. But he was not coming as fast because he was carrying his crippled little brother in his arms. He sat him down on the bottom step, then he sat down and sort of squeezed up against him and pointed to the car.

"There she is, Buddy. Just like I told you upstairs. His brother gave it to him for Christmas and it didn't cost him a cent. And someday I'm going to give you one just like it. You'll see for yourself all the pretty things in the Christmas windows downtown that I've been trying to tell you about."

Paul got out of the car and lifted the lad into the front seat of his car. His shiny-eyed older brother climbed in beside him and the three of them began a memorable holiday ride.

That Christmas Eve Paul learned what it meant to be more blessed to give.

What if you realized your best, highest, noblest, and most inspired dreams?

To recap the first four principles: 1) God is the greatest Giver; 2) You are made in the image and likeness of God; 3) The best giving always includes you as part of the gift; 4) Deciding to give is the first all-important step to giving.

Giving Principle Five

Great people love to give. The world's great givers experience an abundance of their beingness. You can't name a truly great person who wasn't a great giver. Mother Teresa was a great giver, a great fundraiser, and a great inspirer of other givers. She once asked somebody to raise money for a charity and the person asked for funds to travel to the great cities to raise her the money. Mother Teresa advised the person to get the funds with his own power and abilities and walk there if he had to.

Robert G. LeTourneau was a great inventor during the Depression. He created heavy earthmoving equipment. He gave 10 percent of what he earned and then gave 20 percent, then 30. Ultimately during the height of the Depression, he was making more money than anyone else in America. He became a reverse giver—giving away 90 percent because he felt so passionate about helping other people. He kept getting bigger and better ideas and ended up building bridges and machinery for the Panama Canal. He was fond of remarking, "It's not how much of my money I give to God, but how much of God's money I keep for myself."

My neighbors in Newport Beach, California, were Donna and John Crean who founded and created the great Fleetwood International Corporation which makes recreational vehicles and pre-built homes. Together they were super successful and super givers. Donna and I met at a March of Dimes breakfast and she said they gave away half of all they earned—more than a half billion dollars a year. Now that's serious.

Giving Principle Six

Sowing always multiplies at reaping time. Lee Iacocca is known as the auto legend who helped create the Ford Mustang. Iacocca multiplied his success when he became the chairman who saved the Chrysler Corporation from bankruptcy. He created a radical reorganization and took a controversial government loan, which he quickly repaid out of the profits he created on behalf of the company.

Lee courageously wrote an all-time business best seller that sold more than 9 million copies. Lee redefined how we see a modern corporate CEO. Few know, though, that he spearheaded the most successful private fundraising campaign in

U.S. history, generating more than $600 million in contributions to refurbish the Statue of Liberty and revive the adjacent Ellis Island. Lee did it because his parents were Italian immigrants and believed that immigrants made America great.

Robert Schuller says anyone can count the seeds in an apple but only God counts the apples in a seed. One little apple seed can flourish and grow and become 10,000 apples on one tree by the fourth year of the tree's life. A tree theoretically can create countless apple seeds and a potential of feeding everyone everywhere an apple. One seed can reforest and feed the world, and your giving can be that one kind of seed gift that launches a fortune and launches limitless potential in you and in the world.

It's obvious that Lee Iacocca could've gone into retirement after the Ford Motor Company then he could have hung it up and retired after making a colossal success of Chrysler. But instead, what did he do? He said something like, "I've got this giving spirit and I'm going to go make Ellis Island happen again. I'm going to take it and make us all proud and feel good about the nobleness of the immigrants." He could have hung it up after that but remember, dreams don't have deadlines.

You have to have passionate purposefulness to go out and realize your dreams. Will there will be delays and detours and hang ups? Absolutely. But you get to grow and be all that you can be. And like a garden, you have to pluck weeds out because a garden is always being attacked by weeds that try to strangle your dreams. You're bigger than your weeds; you're bigger than your negative thought; you're bigger than your old self-sabotaging behavior.

Giving Principle Seven

Giving always has a multiplying, compounding effect. When Paul Newman passed away in 2008, his Newman's Own company had given away more than $245 million of the net profits and royalties he received to thousands of charities. He started Newman's Own with a single salad dressing in 1982. He inspired Oprah, me, and no doubt thousands more to be givers.

What does it mean? I'm encouraging you to give without an expectation of return because it mysteriously generates a compounding effect in the most unexpected ways and unexpected times and unexpected places.

In the 1960s and '70s, Tina Turner was the most flamboyant and overtly sexual performer in rock and roll. She sang raspy tunes and blues and caressed the microphone seductively. When Tina Turner divorced Ike Turner in 1976, she was left with nothing but the clothes on her back and change in her pocket. She was a hotel maid for three years and was treated well by the hotel manager. When Mick Jagger of the Rolling Stones heard of her plight and remembered what she'd done for him, he immediately hired her to be the Rolling Stones' opening act on their American tour. She embarked on one of the longest and ultimately most successful comebacks in music history.

After she got back on her feet, she bought the hotel where she'd worked for three years. She went up to the general manager and gave him the keys and said, "Because you treated me so well, the hotel is yours." You never know how giving is going to come back to you. Besides that, Tina heard that her friend Lionel Richie was suffering. So she hired him to be her opening act and Lionel got back on his feet and happily and profitably started performing again.

Most people intrinsically know that giving is an investment. Billionaire and founder of the John Templeton Fund, Sir John Marks Templeton said, "Tithing has always been the best investment and pays the greatest returns. When one invests, one can expect a return." Tithing causes a boomerang effect. The parable of the talents says you deserve a 100 percent return, not a cheap miserly bank return. Your tithe will come back to you multiplied, magnetized, and magnified; or as said in the Bible, it will be pressed down, shaken together, and overflowing (Luke 6:38). What is sent out comes back rather automatically.

Just like in the Tina Turner story, paybacks come in different ways at different times and from different people. Giving literally sets up the force field of the universe that spontaneously returns like a well-sent boomerang.

One of my neighbors in Newport Beach is Leigh Steinberg the super-agent to star athletes, and a philanthropist. This is the guy the blockbuster movie *Jerry Maguire* was modeled after, starring Tom Cruise. Lee has negotiated over $2 billion worth of athletic contracts.

Lee inspires every one of his athletes to give; and one year they gave more than $60 million to charitable donations and scholarships. Lee wants to have a positive impact on the world, make it a nicer place, and save the environment. Oh, that all leaders would be so great! Wouldn't it be wonderful if they were all like Lee and gave and inspired others to give?

Giving also launches a multitude of receiving. If you want the best insurance policy to guarantee happiness, get into regular, systematic, heartfelt giving. As mentioned, when Sir John Marks Templeton was asked what was the best and safest investment, his answer was tithing. And don't wait until you get money to tithe. Start now, at once, immediately. Even if you only make $100, give $10 is Templeton's well-founded advice.

Giving 10 percent of what you have puts the universe in your debt. If you put positive energy into the world, positive energy has to come back to you. It's a positive, rebounding system that is infallible, unstoppable. Tithing is the best boomerang system on the planet.

The creator of the restaurant chain Chick-fil-A, Truett Cathy, was a good friend of mine. One time we were sitting at the White House watching several of our Horatio Alger friends become U.S. ambassadors.

I asked Truett, "What is giving to you?" He said, "What's amazing is that it's exhausting trying to give it all away. I have to hire people to help me give it away. Because I've been giving so long, it just keeps automatically and axiomatically multiplying." I agree. It's going to come back bigger and faster than you ever expected.

The goal is to build up your tithing to 10 percent of your gross income. Start small and then you can go to your net income. But if you are unsure or an inexperienced giver, start with pennies, then dollars, then nominal checks. Start with a half of 1 percent, then 1 percent, and keep expanding your giving. You'll soon be amazed at your ever-growing receiving. Bonuses, promotions, windfalls—stuff will happen in expected and not-expected ways. Give a little more with each paycheck until you hit 10 percent.

If your spouse doesn't understand or doesn't want to give, do it out of your own financial resources, your own earnings, your own income. When you really master giving, you'll evolve to a double tithe and perhaps even like LeTourneau, you'll become a reverse tither who gives 90 percent and lives on 10 percent. When the amounts become phenomenal, you can't use it all anyhow. So as your income expands, like LeTourneau's did during the Depression, you may build up and figure out that giving 90 percent will have you vastly richer than giving only 10 percent or no percent.

Someone said, giving starts when you give more than 10 percent, and then the real money multipliers jump into effect. Ralph Waldo Emerson wrote in his essay *Compensation,* which I hope you've read, "Every act rewards itself."

Likewise every gift is its own reward. The universe that sees in secret will shower you with rewards, results, gifts, beneficence, and blessings of every good kind. The best sowing always gets ravaged by life's storms sooner or later—hurricanes, floods, tornadoes, earthquakes, wars, and pestilence. That's why it's necessary to save 10 percent of all you do and earn and create.

You may be familiar with the biblical story of Joseph and his many-colored coat. Joseph interpreted Pharaoh's dreams saying there would be seven years of feast and seven years of famine. During the feast, the Egyptians were to save 20 percent of all their foodstuff. Because of that act, Egypt became the most powerful nation in the world and able to feed everyone within their geographical reach.

Likewise, if you're an enlightened giver, you'll be alerted in time to take advantage of opportunities and warned in time to get out of the way if troubles are coming. What does that mean? If you are a giver and a tither, your inner knower is going to direct you to save more money, resources, or whatever. If you have that little intuitive inner knowing, listen to it, because when you live a principled life, you become ever more enlightened.

Giving Principle Eight

Principle eight is *the law of reciprocity.* When you give or do something nice for another person, it stimulates or triggers that person to generally do a similar kindness or activity back to you. No one wants to feel obligated or indebted. Rather, the great self-interest-oriented leadership says give yourself away and put the universe in your debt. My friend Bob Proctor says of me, "You have to get up early in the morning to out-give Mark Victor Hansen."

I love to give, contribute, and serve greatly. It feels good; it works; it generates forever better results in my life; and in my experience, it creates unfolding possibilities. It leads to a brightness of the future that is compellingly, inviting, fascinating, desirable to me and all with whom I share my life. Each of us should share a little—that way a lot would be shared, everyone would be better off, and no one would be worse off. And as far as I'm concerned, we can make the world work for 100 percent of humanity.

The fulfilled life is a giving life. Visualize yourself as a cheerful, happy, joyous giver. Even before you are one, don't make the mistake of thinking that you have to be a millionaire in order to give. There are plenty of things to share besides money, and many of them are just as valuable if not more valuable. For example, share and give your time, experiences, professional services, and most definitely your prayers. Being a giver literally expands your very soul.

As Quaker missionary Stephen Grellet said, "I shall pass through this world but once. Any good therefore that I can do or any kindness that I can show to any human being, let me do it now. Let me not defer or neglect it, for I shall not pass this way again." The world can be made healthy, safe, and prosperous for 100 percent of humankind. This has never been possible before. The resources are here. The people are here. You're here. I'm here. If the rest the world buys into this model of giving, they will make a bundle—and give it away. It is said that more than $25 trillion dollars will be given away in this decade and expanded in future decades to over $100 trillion. It's hard to imagine what's possible, but let's give it a try.

Marilyn Van Derbur, a former Miss America, tells a great classic story. During World War II, both sides agreed they would not destroy churches. But in Italy, bombshells from the enemy unfortunately destroyed not only a church but also the statue of Christ in front of the church. When people got together and American soldiers were contributing their time, effort, and energy to putting things back together, they came upon the Cristo statue, which was severely damaged. It was made out of Carrara marble, considered the prettiest and the best of alabaster Italian marbles.

They decided to try and put the statue back together. They glued it and polished it, but the hands of the statue were demolished. They thought about it, and that night called for a group church congregational meeting, including the Americans. They wondered if they should have another set of hands made or just put a new statement in front of the marble statue of Christ. They chose a new statement:

The only eyes God has are yours.
The only heart God has to beat with is yours.
And the only hands the Master has to do
masterful giving with, are yours.

LEADERS AND LEADERSHIP

Many people, and probably you're one of them, reach a point in their lives where they develop leadership, which is defined as character and competence with expertise in a given subject area. The subject may be one that you feel emotionally attached to, an area that is directly connected to your lifelong dreams, or may simply be a profession or skill that you've mastered over the course of your career. In any case, it's very important to bring what you've learned to the world by becoming the leader of leaders and a mentor to others.

I really want you to be a visionary leader who leads. You now have all this eclectic wisdom to put together, package, blueprint, and see what you can do to make a significant, impactful, important, and lasting difference. If you want to do something better, teach someone else how to do it and you'll learn at a deeper depth; you'll learn to communicate it eloquently and effectively.

There's a short story about two famous orators from ancient Greece, Pericles and Demosthenes. There was a difference between them. After Pericles spoke, people said, "He moved my soul." After Demosthenes spoke, people said, "Let's march. Let's take action. Let's go to war. Let's win!" The difference between those two speakers is a difference between management and leadership. It's a difference between information and inspiration. Most importantly, it's a difference between talking to people and helping them start to do something, something that's actionable. That difference is vital to everyone today because when you become a leader of leaders and an inspiration to others, you automatically become a leader and inspiration to yourself.

We've talked about my friend Dr. Norman Vincent Peale, author of *The Power of Positive Thinking.* He once said to me, "Who leaves the motivational seminar most motivated? Of course, the motivator!" It's obvious what being a leader can do for other people; but being a leader can also do tremendous things for you, especially later in life.

Examples: Moses was on the run from the law and living in the middle of the wilderness. When God appeared to him in a burning bush, He announced that Moses would lead his people from slavery to freedom. Moses was by no means eager to undertake this task. He actually tried to talk God out of it. Why? Moses doubted himself. But God uses ordinary people to do extraordinary things.

You may be thinking, *Well, that's me. I'm an ordinary person who wants to do an extraordinary thing.* Once you decide to do so, your relatives may make negative comments like, "Who do you think you are? You've never done anything like that. You think you can do that? Are you crazy? Come on, snap out of it. Go back and get a job, do something normal, be a regular person."

When God approached him, Moses was a guy who felt safe; he was an 83-year-old shepherd. His family was grown and he was living in what we call Ethiopia today. He in essence said to God that there has to be somebody more qualified to do this task.

But leadership is not only about qualifications. The qualifications for leadership develop once the actions toward leadership are taken. I encourage you to put your boots on. Decide to be strong. Put some spirit in your spine. Decide what it is you can do to make a positive difference in your family, your community, at your workplace—the world around you.

Moses became the leader of leaders by doing things that leaders do. He needed to be for himself first by being what he needed to be for others. To serve others greatly for the sake of serving, love for the sake of loving, care for the sake of caring. Then the leader in you starts to emerge.

A leader takes a stand, and you command from your stand. Sometimes a stand is not going to be popular. Most leaders are doubted. Most leaders have to look around for like-minded supporters because there can't be a leader unless there are followers.

Let's go to another example—Ulysses S. Grant. He was a complete failure at everything as long as he was working only for himself. But when the Civil War erupted, he rejoined the army and was put in a leadership position. First a small one. That's how leadership starts. You start small and you progressively get tall. Quickly he was assigned larger and larger tasks. Once Grant took on responsibility and leadership, he became much larger as a person in every respect. Grant found qualities in himself that he never suspected he had. In fact he might not have had them if he hadn't become a leader.

Let's look at a leader who came on the political scene late in life, Ronald Reagan. Reagan had been an actor and a good one. At 72 years young, he became President of the United States after having been governor of California. By becoming a leader of others, you bring the most out of yourself; take advantage of that opportunity to the maximum.

You may already be in a position of leadership. You may be the owner of a business; you may supervise a group of employees in a company. You may be a physician or an attorney with patients, clients, and staff members depending on you. If that's the case, your leadership role is already clear and well-defined. All I want you to do now is ask yourself, *How do I multiply it? What would it take for me to tenfold or hundredfold my leadership role? What's possible if I got rid of my own self-sabotaging doubts and lack of belief?*

EXPAND YOURSELF

What is possible if we think leadership is an infinitely expandable balloon with our name on it and we just keep blowing more air into it? Blowing your leader self into it will expand it. I really want you to think what it would be like if you expanded yourself tenfold or hundredfold financially, spiritually, emotionally, and most of all as a leader.

There are other situations in which leadership potential is more subtle. You may be a freelance or self-employed person with no official leadership responsibility. You may be a retired person or someone starting out in a new career. The surprising thing is that none of that really matters. There's always, always, always an opportunity for you to be a leader.

The country is desperately short of leaders. Whether in the workplace, politics, or your community. There are leadership opportunities in your career, family, bowling team, and in the classroom, for examples. Most especially there are leadership roles in our society that need leaders on a voluntary basis. You could coach a sport, teach a class, volunteer in a hospital or library, tutor a student, organize a book club, become a docent in a museum, head a philanthropy, or be the fundraiser of all fundraisers.

When I was writing *The Aladdin Factor,* one of the people Jack and I interviewed was the fundraiser of all fundraisers at that time. A lady at Stanford University called all the alumni and she personally, with just a telephone call, raised $1 billion for that school. As a sidebar on that school, you may or may not know this classic story we have in a *Chicken Soup* book about Leland Stanford and his wife, Jane. Their son had died and they went to Harvard University to speak to the president. They sat outside the president's office all day long. Because they were wearing farm clothes and looked like they were just working class people, at 5:30 in the afternoon, they were taken into the office and he says, "What do you want?"

Stanford introduced himself and introduced his wife. He said, "What does it take to build a building?"

The president said, "I think a hundred thousand dollars."

"What does it take to build a whole campus?"

The president said, "Five million dollars."

"Well, had you not had us out there all day cooling our heels, I would have given you ten million dollars so you would have had twice as much to expand Harvard."

So Mr. and Mrs. Stanford left Harvard that day because they had been belittled. Mr. Stanford, who was the great American railroad tycoon, built a campus that matched and surpassed Harvard and other rivals. The biggest land holding he had was in a small place called Palo Alto in California, and there he built Stanford University—which is now one of the most prestigious universities in the country.

A real leader is nice to everybody. There are no little people, only different people. A real leader sees potential in everyone and sees more potential in them than anyone else sees.

WORTHY FUNDRAISING

I'd like you to think about being a leader as a fundraiser. Decide that sometime during your life you're going to be the fundraiser for the charity or philanthropy of your choice. This is how we teach you how: If you stepped into an elevator with billionaire Bill Gates and you had fifteen seconds to tell him what your philanthropy of choice is, and he would give you a million dollars, what would it be?

At one of our millionaire summits, a lady who was exceedingly pregnant stood up as the first person to answer our question. She said, "Here's what I'd say. 'Mr. Gates, you see I'm very pregnant. I know you and Melinda have two kids you totally love. Would you please take your hand and place it on my stomach. I'm adopted, and in America there are one million nine hundred thousand kids who are born without a real, loving family and need to be adopted. So, Mr. Gates, I'd like you to give me a million dollars so I could be the spokesperson for adopting children and make sure that every child is adopted into a loving family.'" What she said was so good, so tenderhearted, so kind and genuine.

There are also many websites devoted to the opportunities for volunteer leadership and mentoring. I have no doubt that you can find outlets that suit your talents, skills, interests, and capabilities, On the other hand, there doesn't have to be a perfect fit. If you're looking too closely for one, you should ask yourself whether you're really looking for ways to avoid leadership. Zig Ziglar calls this paralysis by analysis.

Just search for the word "mentoring" on the Internet and you may be startled as you quickly discover how many places there are to mentor. You've probably been mentored, and now it's time for you to share your wisdom, insights, enlightenment, and your life experience—as you do, you're going to grow exponentially.

LEADERSHIP AND MENTORING

I want to share with you a story about Jaime Escalante. You may have seen the movie *Stand and Deliver.* If you haven't, go out of your way to watch it. It's good. Jaime got into the computer business, made his fortune, and retired. Then he realized that he had a great, inspiring teacher who had mentored him and turned him on to math and science so he could make his fortune. From that realization, he decided to go back into the Hispanic ghetto where he was from and teach kids a love of mathematics and a love of learning.

A leader who leads chooses to be a visionary. Jaime went back to the school and at first all the kids ridiculed him. They didn't know where he was from, and they didn't know that he had five Rolls Royces. One of the kids said, "You think you're so cool. Teachers don't get paid anything. See that car out there that's got flames all over it? That's mine. I flip hamburgers at McDonald's."

Jaime responded, "The problem, my friend, is that if you don't learn what I'm going to teach you, you're gonna be flipping McDonald's hamburgers for the rest of your life." And he eventually turned the class around, just like in another movie starring Sidney Poitier, *To Sir With Love.* He took a leadership role in a group of students who were undisciplined and arrogant and made a difference in their lives.

You can choose to mentor and give back in education, government, business, medicine, law, anywhere you have an interest. There's a leader inside you; a leader desperate to be released. I'm giving you permission today to release your great leadership. The world needs you. Your family needs you. The business, industry, or association you're in needs you; and most importantly, the future needs you to live up to your leadership ability. There's more in you than you ever thought.

If you want to really get into the topic of leadership, study, read, and listen to John Maxwell's books and tapes. He will get you going. He has devoted many years of his life doing nothing but thinking about and teaching leadership. He is a master at making leadership principles seem easy and effortless so you can say, "Leadership is the truth of me." That's what I want you to understand—leadership is who you are and what you're about. At some level, somewhere, sometime, somehow, I look forward to meeting you and hearing your leadership breakthrough story.

There are two sides to the coin when talking about leadership. We've talked about being a leader yourself, but there's also immense benefit in finding a leader or mentor to help guide you. It's a big mistake to think being mentored can only happen in the early part of your life or in the early part of your career. You can be a leader and you can also benefit by supporting a leader and being a follower, or becoming a mentee to a leader as you emerge in leadership skills.

SEVEN TYPES OF MENTORS

I believe there are seven types of mentors everyone needs: financial, health, relationship, social, spiritual, intellectual, and an overall life guide.

First you need a *financial mentor*, or two. You need a mentor to help you with your earning power. There are two parts to finances: earning power and net worth. In *Think and Grow Rich,* Napoleon Hill wrote the following classic poem:

> *I bargained with Life for a penny*
> *And Life would pay no more,*
> *However I begged at evening*
> *When I counted my scanty store.*
> *For Life is a fair employer,*
> *He gives you what you ask,*
> *But once you have set the wages,*

Why, you must bear the task.
I worked for a menial's hire,
Only to learn, dismayed,
That any wage I had asked of Life,
Life would have willingly paid.

Everyone is somewhere on the financial ladder. Most of us are somewhere in the middle. You get to go as high on that earning power ladder as you want. If you're earning $50,000, you ought to write down that you want twice that much. If you're earning $100,000, write down you want to earn $250,000, etc. Keep expanding the possibility because consciousness is the key.

I want to be your financial mentor right this minute and say what I learned from W. Clement Stone. If you make $100,000 a year, understand it's conceptual, so you need to contract it and figure out how to make $100,000 a month, then you want to make $100,000 a week, then $100,000 a day, then $100,000 an hour, then $100,000 a minute. Remember, it's all consciousness. Set your mind on a task and then the task is self-fulfilled.

The second part is net worth. Dr. Ken Dychtwald said your minimum net worth should be $2 million when you decide to retire at 65, 72, or whenever or if you retire. You want to have a minimum so you're debt-free, stress-free, and set free.

The second mentor you need is a *health mentor.* You have to think healthy and keep telling yourself you're healthy, and repeat that until it becomes a truth to you. Constantly build up your immune system by eating healthy and having the finest nutrition available to you. You read earlier about being healthy not only in terms of the food you eat but also in terms of nutritional supplements and detoxing your system. To be healthy, you have to exercise; in my opinion, six days a week. It's good to have a variety of exercises you do at different times and different places; cross train yourself too.

The third is a *relationship mentor.* Historically, a grandmother or grandfather used to sit in a rocking chair and solve everybody's problems. Today that role has been taken over by psychotherapists, psychologists, and psychiatrists; it's become the province of the paid professional. But maybe you can develop enough soul depth that you can solve a lot of people's relationship problems. You can be the equivalent of Solomon in your family and solve some of the issues that arise—saving a lot of money and time. Do I believe that you ought to have someone to bounce ideas off regarding your emotional needs? The answer is yes. Everyone needs someone who really cares and knows you at a soul level, a core level, at the essence of your being and is willing to discuss with you how to make your relationships work.

You need a *social mentor* because there are important social skills to be learned such as simple etiquette. Many people don't even know the basics like not chewing gum when doing business. Find someone who has elegance, class, and operates with dignity. Embrace that so you learn proper language skills, so when you open your mouth you're saying what is appropriate and then you will be able to socialize how and when you want to.

Our minister and his wife and my wife and I took dance classes in our middle life years. I have to admit the other people in the dance class were younger, but that was irrelevant. Dreams don't have deadlines. Age only matters if it matters to you. And I'm asking you to shuck that attitude, because it doesn't matter. It is something people impose on themselves and put deadlines on their dreams. Shoot down the deadlines that say tell you, I can't learn how to dance, I can't learn how to be articulate, I can't learn a new language, whatever your can't is.

In one of our early *Chicken Soup* books, there is a story about a fourth grade teacher who had all the kids write down everything they thought they couldn't do. Then she told them to crinkle up the paper and throw it into the wastebasket. She carried it outside to the back of the schoolyard and the students watched as she dug a two-foot deep grave, dumped the paper into it, lit it on fire, and covered it up. Their can'ts were burned and buried.

Everyone has things we think we can't do socially, financially, in our relationships, health, spirit, intellect, and our overall life. I'm asking you to write down all your can'ts, light them on fire, cremate them, then bury them deep.

A *spiritual mentor* is important as you go through life. If your priest, minister, or rabbi isn't getting to the core of your soul and just doesn't make your whole spirit sing and zing, then find somebody who does. Find the place that has the music, message, insight, and wisdom you need to do life abundantly—that stimulates you to the core of your being to grow.

You also need an *intellectual mentor.* Oprah says two things made her great. One, she journals every day. She says she was born with no voice, no money, no time, no connections.

Well, that's true of all of us; we were all born naked, helpless, and ignorant. She says now, "I have a big voice, big money, big interests, and a big message that I want to share with the world." Two, she reads two books a week. I encourage you to read what will make you deeper, richer, more meaningful, and can help you make wise decisions about more issues.

The seventh mentor you need is an *overall life guide*. What does that mean? That means someone who helps you work with the blueprint, the pattern of integrity called your life.

How far do you want to go? How big do you want to be? What do you want to discover about yourself? What challenges are you willing to face? It's not just for Sir Edmund Hillary to want to climb his Mount Everest. Everyone is coded a DNA and RNA at birth to have some challenge, some conquest we're supposed to do.

I want to reforest the planet and I want to end illiteracy, because my parents were language illiterate and I saw the slavery of illiteracy. But what is it that *you* want to do? I want to house the unhoused. I have done some very interesting things with Habitat for Humanity. I told the founder, Millard Fuller, that One Minute Millionaire wanted to raise a million dollars as well as get a million people to help build Habitat houses. It's a clean, well-thought-out operation. And what's amazing to me is that everyone cries when the keys are given to the family the night after the home is built. The workers cry because they helped people who couldn't help themselves or never had an opportunity to have a nice roof over their head. I think everybody likes to come out to an old-fashioned barn raising where you roll up your sleeves and contribute. I've never had one person turn me down when I asked for help for Habitat for Humanity.

Do you have someone who can help you determine your integrity pattern, your blueprint of life? Can you talk it through with someone? In his seminars, Jack and I sit eyeball to eyeball with each attendee and keep asking, "What do you want? What do you want? What do you want?" Most start out saying something like, "I want my right livelihood. I want my ideal spouse. I want my kids to graduate from college." But after ten or so of that same question, the answers start to come from the depth of the person's soul.

A 67-year-old doctor in Hawaii in one of our seminars came up to me afterward, and with tears in his eyes said, "In all my training, this two minutes has meant more to me than anything else because no one ever asked at the quick of my soul what I really wanted in life."

Another similar life guide example is when a dentist attended one of my seminars and he said, "I never heard that question; no one ever asked me what I wanted. Last week I drilled through the side of a guy's mouth who wasn't insured and it cost me $480,000. Now suddenly your question gets to the core of my being and I get it—I never wanted to be a dentist." He continued, "My mother kept saying, 'My son the dentist, my son the dentist.' I did this for her. This isn't what I want to do." And then he told me what he wanted to do, his right livelihood, his passionate and purposeful place to be in life.

We need an overall life guide.

And then as a bonus—we also need a *tech mentor.* This mentor may be your kids or grandkids who help you get and stay literate on a computer and/or smart phone.

The trick is having someone in your life who can help you fulfill your dreams, which is not the opposite of being a leader yourself. It's about the recognition that you can't do everything on your own. It's the commitment to finding people who've been down your path before who can help point you in a right direction.

Leadership is about self-leadership. It's about giving you a new directional compass, giving you a new North Star to bounce off of. The visionary leader inside you is waiting to be unleashed. Come out of the cocoon now; the cocoon is open. Dry your wings in the light of day. It's warm and it's sunny and it's beautiful, and the world never needed you to become a self-leader who could be a leader of others more than it does now.

CHAPTER 11

LOOK FORWARD

Dennis Tito was a major paradigm shifter. A paradigm is a shift in our awareness, our consciousness, concept, or idea. At 60 years young, Tito was an American tycoon, founder of the Wilshire Fund, who invested $20 million of his own money to pay his fare to fly into space with the Russians. He proved, like Senator John Glenn did earlier, that life's dreams aren't over because you're starting to mature. Dreams don't have deadlines.

Tito further proved that there's always a way. I want to repeat that principle: There's always a way you can avail yourself to opportunity; whenever you're ready, it's ready for you at any age. Money freedom creates time freedom which creates relationship freedom which creates genius freedom. Tito had the freedom of choice, even to fly in space. It was said in the old days, "If we can land a man on the moon, we can do anything!" Since that first commercial spaceflight in 2001, we've seen individual breakthroughs of this paradigm.

Earlier in the book you read about two timelines in your life. One was a simple chronology that took place over the years. The other was a wish list for your hopes and dreams, some of which may have come to fruition, while others are yet to be realized.

As you look at those two timelines now, I hope they look rather different from when you created them. Specifically, I hope that the second one about your dreams looks not like a record of something that's over and done, but a snapshot of a work very much in progress.

The key purpose of this book has been to provide you with both the inspiration and dedication so you will put up the perspiration to get to the destination with some practical tools for completing the work that's in progress.

In his final chapter, I'd like to suggest and even ask you to see the timelines of your life even more differently. We tend to think of our lives as storylines, as linear narratives with a beginning, a middle, and an end. But suppose you look at your life in an entirely different way. I think of it as a jigsaw puzzle or as a landscape painting or even as a dream in which time has much more fluid and flexible meaning than it does in the everyday world of deadlines and due dates. And by the way, I think deadlines and due dates are exciting because they keep us motivated to complete projects before the deadline hits.

One of the most interesting alternatives to the linear view of our lives is the metaphor of a maze, or more precisely a labyrinth. There's an important difference between a maze and a labyrinth. A maze is a puzzle in which there are lots of false starts and dead ends. You get lost in the maze and often have to backtrack, sometimes all the way to the very beginning. A labyrinth, on the other hand, is a complicated, twisting, circuitous pathway. All you have to do is keep going and you get to the end, although it may take you a long time to reach the end of the labyrinth. But the only way you can fail to reach your goal is if you stop trying. That's the way life is—we must persist.

When I took my family to Europe, we went to the Hampton Court Palace of King Henry VIII. That place has the greatest and biggest and most exquisite labyrinth in the world and it takes over an hour to go through it because the hedge bushes are 20 feet high. There are times when the kids got ahead of me and I couldn't see them. It scared me a little bit, but I knew my wife was waiting at the end and she'd take care of the kids. Plus, there was a guy in a tower overlooking the labyrinth so everybody was safe inside. I thought it was a neat little test of whether people tough it out and make it to the end. Well, you've almost made it to the end of this book—but we're not done yet.

If you know that your dreams don't have deadlines and if your goals are bigger and your soul goals are in the place of your right livelihood, some interesting and important things can happen and still get done.

During World War II, Russia was invaded by Germany for four years. At one point an American officer was sent to speak with a commander of the Russian forces. The American asked how many men Russia thought it would take to defeat the invaders. The Russian said he didn't know. The American asked how many tanks would it take? How many planes? How much money would it cost? The Russian said he didn't know.

The American was perplexed, "Frankly, it doesn't seem like you know much about what's going on."

The Russian shook his head and said, "I know a lot. I know that if I give you a number of how many troops it requires, it would turn out to require more than that. If I tell you how many tanks or planes or how much money, it will be more than that. So I'm going to say I don't know those things. But there is one thing for sure I know."

"And what's that?" the American asked.

"I know that we will win."

I'm not suggesting that we should look at our lives as a war against an invading army. But I am suggesting that you should keep your eye on the prize rather than on the twisting roads or the detours along the way. Russia did win.

If you know any Russian history, you know it has the harshest, coldest winters in the world. The weather beat Napoleon; and had Hitler been a better student and studied his history, perhaps he would have done something different. Russia's inclement weather froze the oil in the Nazi war tanks, and the ill-clothed Nazi soldiers froze to death.

If you haven't achieved everything you've hoped for by this point in your life, it's not too late. You can keep moving forward. Robert Schuller said, "God's delays aren't God's denials." Maybe you stopped moving or stopped believing. If you stopped trusting in your own abilities, I want you to shake off that distrust in the presence of the Higher Power who is always there to help you. Never stop hoping, and never stop moving. Just keep going.

There is an old joke about a man down on his luck so he prayed to win the lottery, but nothing happened. He started getting angry and shouting at God. God said, "Go halfway with Me and buy a lottery ticket." We have to do our part.

FULL RELEASE OF POTENTIAL

Allow me to briefly example some of the full release of potential that I've seen, watched, and thought about. I hope you'll think a little bit about it too.

Another one of our books is *Chicken Soup for the American Soul.* After 9-11, all of America was shell-shocked because of the terrorist attacks. A lot of stories were sent to us that touched the quick of our being when we read them. There was a story of a 5-year-old girl named Sonali. Her dad was an environmental lawyer, as good as it gets. Alan Beaven worked hard, but he knew the principle about taking a sabbatical every seven years. He told his wife, Kimi, and his son and his daughter that they were going on a sabbatical after his assignment in California; they lived in Boston. That morning, he kissed his wife and kids goodbye and went to the airport.

He's so enamored with this family that at the airport he calls one more time and says, "Kimi, I'm going out to California to get our pot of gold, then I'll be back and we get to go on our little sabbatical."

She said, "Honey, you are our pot of gold. You can't go get our pot of gold."

Then he boarded Flight 93. Kimi is watching TV later that day and it said the flight from Boston enroute to California, Flight 93, went into the ground in Pennsylvania and everybody was instantaneously killed.

The passengers on that flight fought back against the terrorists. Rather than the plane crashing into the White House or the capital building, it crashed into the ground in a clear area where there were no homes and no one except those on the plane were killed.

When little Sonali came home from school that day, she was effervescent joyful. She didn't know that her daddy had been killed by terrorists that day and mommy didn't want to break her euphoria, so she let her play for an hour. Then finally she held her daughter's hands and told her what was wrong as they sat together. She said, "If I never hear crying and wailing like that again, it would be too soon." It was way too painful, way too much anguish, way too much grief for one heart to bear.

Later that day her big brother, Chris, said to Sonali, "Do you know where daddy is?"

She said, "Yeah, Daddy's at work."

"What do you mean, Daddy's at work?"

"Daddy's at work. He's out defending the angels." She knew what had happened to her dad.

This little girl, Sonali, sings like an angel and she sang at her daddy's funeral. Then she was invited to sing in Pennsylvania. Then the governor of California invited her to sing one more time, because at five years old, she could raise the spirits of America like nobody else. On the flight to California, a flight attendant said, "I've heard your story and I'd like you to sing to everybody on the plane, because America couldn't be in any more pain than it is now. Would you be willing to do that?"

She said, "Yeah."

"First, do you want to walk down the aisles and see how many people there are?"

"Yeah."

She tenderly held Sonali's hand and they walked up and down the aisles as she looked and nodded at everyone.

When they were at the front again, the attendant asked, "How many people do you think are on this plane?"

"Oh, over a thousand," Sonali said.

"Well, do you feel strong enough and secure enough to sing into the P.A. system?"

"Yeah, I could do that."

Sonali sang a song that melted everyone's hearts and souls, including the pilot and copilot. They said they couldn't hold back the tears.

The flight attendant asked, "Sonali, how did you have the courage to do that?"

She said, "My daddy said he'd always hold my hand when he was living, and I know things haven't changed just because he's on the other side."

What am I saying to you? That's a paradigm shift.

PREPARE FOR PARADIGM SHIFTS

We're in a greatest time of paradigm shifts in human history. There have never been paradigm shifts like there are now. I'm old enough to remember when 78 records became 33 and 33s became audiotapes and audiotapes became CDs. Then there was Napster and now every type of music imagined is available on the Internet. A paradigm shift was when we went from horse and buggy transportation to the car. In the old days we only had cyclical shifts—today we have structural changes that can only goof you up if you don't expect them or aren't prepared for them.

If you are a self-leader and a tither, if you are a giver who is resolute in your giving, you will be alerted in times of opportunity. And there is more opportunity than ever before. That's why this book is titled *Dreams Don't Have Deadlines.* Don't self-sabotage yourself. If you buy into the worst, into the lowest, and if someone prays into your fear, you'll shut down and be immobilized, stifled and condemned to living less than your full potential.

Find a mentor who makes your heart sing, stabs your spirit alive, and gets your spirit to stand in command. Decide that you are not going to have deadlines on your dreams—rather, you're going to realize your dreams not only for yourself but for all of humanity. The future is big and it's bright and it's wonderful; with a paradigm shift you have a future that is so irresistibly compelling that you are driven toward it.

You have to be willing to speak from the peak and share your dreams and visions with other people. You have to be willing to be strong in spirit, and strong sometimes for others who are weak or feeling vulnerable. You can be the one people turn to when they need somebody with courage. Courage is a French word that means strength of heart. I'm asking you to work on the strength of your heart and be more courageous than you've ever been.

I'm asking you to look forward and be willing to explore paradigm shifts in awareness, consciousness, concept, idea, and habits. You will either crumble on yourself and have weak habits or decide to get strong and courageous.

As my colleague and friend Zig Ziglar said, "When you're easy on yourself, life's hard on you; but when you're hard on yourself, life's easy on you." When you go after the disciplines to make you strong and healthy, all the principles we've talked about, you will be resolute and have insight that's out of sight.

Remember, write down ten outrageous goals that are going to help you become all that you can be in a time when we need leadership in every area of endeavor. Strive to be strong in your family, company, opportunities, and for your future. Then expand your reach from local to regional, state, national, and then wrap it around the world.

You may want to consider the responsibility of caring for the ecology. We live in a fragile ecology that's only ten miles high as far as you can breathe and ten miles deep. At some level from a space point of view, our problems are little and we're little. But from a human point of view, our problems are big and there are many needs that have human urgency attached to them.

I think that in this decade we can feed all of humanity. That's a paradigm shift I wrote down thirty years ago when I was apprenticing with Buckminster Fuller and he was my mentor. I wrote down ten outrageous goals. Did I know it was possible? Well, a few years ago we worked with Campbell's soup company and we raised enough food from donations to feed 15 million people.

There are possibilities that you know of, some aches in your heart, and pain in your soul. Something is irking your conscious and there is a pinprick in the spirit of your being that says you want to do something about it. Write it down and then go to town to get it done. Use all the inspiration I shared with you in this book.

I want you to have a new destination and new dedication. I want you to let the perspiration flow toward the realization of that destination with zip, vim, and vigor. I can't tell you how it's going to come to pass. I also can't tell you what structural things are going to happen; but I *can* tell you that the world needs you to be a leader at levels you didn't expect you had.

I want to conclude with a couple of stories all packed together and then wrap it up in a bow to share it with you.

Ross Perot was a presidential candidate in 1992 and 1996. Before that, though, you may not know how he was the top salesman at IBM; and in 17 days he sold so much he earned $287,000. The chairman of the board told him he made too much, and fired him. So Perot borrowed $1,000 from his wife and started Electronic Data Systems (EDS). He knocked on eighty doors to make a sale—they all said no.

I teach in *The Aladdin Factor* that if somebody says no, you just keep saying next, next, next. Perot eventually knocked on a door and got a $4 million order for his new business. He went on to build a great company.

I want to conclude with one more heartfelt story from a *Chicken Soup* book. It's called All the Good Things.

In a third grade class I taught at Saint Mary's School in Morris, Minnesota, all thirty-four of my students were dear to me. But Mark Eklund was one in a million. He was neat in appearance, he had a happy-to-be-alive attitude, and even made the occasional mischievousness delightful. Mark talked incessantly. I reminded him again and again that talking without permission was not acceptable.

What impressed me so much, though, was his sincere response. Every time I had to correct him for misbehaving, he said, "Thank you for correcting me, Sister." I didn't know what to make of it at first. But before long I became accustomed to hearing it many, many times a day. One morning my patience was growing thin when Mark talked once too often. I made the novice teacher's mistake. I looked at Mark and said, "If you say one more word, I'm going to tape your mouth shut."

It wasn't ten seconds later Chuck blurted out, "Mark's talking again, Sister." I had asked the students to help me watch Mark, and since I'd stated the punishment in front of the class, I had to act on it. I remember the scene as if it had occurred this morning. I walked to my desk very deliberately, opened a drawer, pulled out the roll of masking tape, and without saying a word, I proceeded to Mark's desk, tore off two pieces of tape, and made a big X with tape over his mouth.

When returning to the front of the room, I glanced at Mark to see how he was doing. He winked at me. That did it. I started laughing. The entire class cheered as I walked back to Mark's desk, removed the tape, and shrugged my shoulders. His first words were, "Thanks for correcting me, Sister."

The end of the year I was asked to teach junior high school math. The years had flown by and before I knew it Mark was in my classroom again. He was more handsome than ever and just as polite. He listened carefully to my instruction in New Math, so he did not talk as much in the ninth grade.

One Friday things didn't feel right. We'd worked hard on new concept all week and I sensed the students were growing frustrated with themselves and edgy with one another. I had to stop this crankiness before it got out of hand, so I asked them to list the names of all the other students in the class on two sheets of paper leaving a space between each name. Then I told them to think of the nicest thing they'd say about each of their classmates and write it down. It took the remainder of the class period to finish the assignment, but as students left the room, each one handed me the paper.

Mark said, "Thank you for teaching me, Sister, have a good weekend." That Saturday I wrote down the name of each student on a separate sheet of paper and listed what everyone else had to say about that classmate. On Monday, I gave each student his or her list, some were two pages. Before long, the entire class was smiling and happy.

"Really?" I heard someone whisper. Another student said, "I never knew that meant anything to him." And, "I didn't know somebody liked me so much." No one ever mentioned those papers again in class, and I never knew if they discussed them after class or with their parents. But it didn't much matter. The exercise had accomplished its purpose. The students were happy with themselves and one another again.

The group of students moved on. Several years later after I'd returned from vacation, my parents met me at the airport. During the drive home, Mother asked the usual questions about the trip, the weather, my experience in general. Then there was a slight lull in the conversation. Mother gave Dad a sideways glance and simply said, "Dad." My father cleared his throat. He said, "The Eklund's called last night."

"Really? I haven't heard from them in several years. I wonder how Mark's doing."

Dad responded quietly. "Mark was killed in Vietnam. The funeral's tomorrow. His parents asked if you'd like to attend." To this day I can still point to the exact spot on Interstate 494 where Dad told me about Mark.

I had never seen a service man in a military coffin before. Mark looked so handsome, so mature. All I could think at the moment was, *Mark, I'd give all the masking tape in the world if only you could talk to me.* The church was packed with Mark's friends. Chuck's sister sang "The Battle Hymn of the Republic." Why did it have to rain the day of the funeral, it was difficult enough at the graveside.

The pastor said the usual prayers, a bugler played "Taps." Then one by one those who loved Mark walked by his coffin and sprinkled it with holy water. I was the last one to bless the coffin. As I stood there, one of the soldiers who had acted as pallbearer came up to me and asked, "Were you Mark's math teacher?" I nodded. As I continued to stare at the coffin, he said, "Mark talked about you all the time."

After the funeral, most of Mark's former classmates headed to Chuck's farmhouse for lunch. Mark's mother and father were there, obviously waiting for me. His dad said, "We want to show you something." The father took a wallet out of his pocket. "They found this on Mark when he was killed. We thought you might recognize it."

From the billfold he carefully removed two worn pieces of notebook paper that had obviously been taped together, folded, and refolded many times. I knew without looking that those papers were the ones on which I had listed all the good things that each of Mark's classmates had said about him.

"Thank you so much for doing that," Mark's mother said. "As you can see, Mark treasured it."

Mark's classmates started gathering around us. Chuck smiled rather sheepishly and said, "I still have my list in the top drawer of my desk at home." John's wife said, "John asked me to put his in our wedding album." "I have mine too," Marilyn said, "it's in my diary." Then Vicki, another classmate, reached in her pocketbook and took out her wallet and showed her worn, frazzled list to the group. "I carry it with me at all times everywhere I go," Vicki said, without batting an eyelash. "I think we all saved our lists."

That's when I finally sat down and cried. I cried for Mark and I cried for all his friends who'd never see him again.

Let me tie this story up by saying that throughout the book I've asked you to have a list. A list of who you are, who you want to be, what you want to have, where you want to go, who you want to go with, and what you want to do—because dreams don't have deadlines. All you need is a list that is irresistibly compelling to you. I don't know how it will come to pass, but poof, it will come to be because your dreams don't have deadlines.

CONCLUSION

We've covered so much in *Dreams Don't Have Deadlines.* We started with the curtain rising again—and the curtain is going to continue to rise and rise and rise over you.

You've read that you ought to have some goals; you ought to have some fun; you ought to have some health; you ought to have some wealth; you ought to have some spiritual aware-ness; and you have to sprinkle in a little bit of connection so you start meeting and greeting new people. You ought to smile more often too.

As you advance into these levels of new awareness, you get to start giving at levels you have maybe never given before. Then you can become a leader among leaders—a visionary leader who leads. You are strong enough to lead no matter how the paradigm shifts. There will be structural changes, but you are courageous enough to tackle each one you face.

And when you start to predict the future—just like you know that summer comes after spring and fall after sum-mer—and you can see down the road that there's going to be some major paradigm shifts, you're going to use the infor-mation you've just learned here to make your life good, better, and then make better the best. You're going to have an extraordinary future!

Never again will there be a dream in you that has a dead-line. You're going to add dreams to your dreams and visions to your visions. Your heart's going to sing as you go into a glo-rious, wonderful, and perfect future. You will make the roads smoother, better, and more wonderful for you and anyone who gets close to you.

On behalf of Nightingale-Conant and myself, we congratulate you for being on an uplifted path that's enlightened and filled with wonderment, overflowing with good for yourself and all around you.

And remember, my friend, *dreams don't have deadlines.*

ABOUT THE AUTHOR

Mark Victor Hansen is probably best known as the coauthor for the *Chicken Soup for the Soul* book series and brand, setting world records in book sales, with over 500 million books sold to date.

Mark has also worked his way into a worldwide spotlight as a sought-after keynote speaker and entrepreneurial marketing maven, creating a stream of successful people who have created massive success for themselves through Mark's unique teachings and wisdom. With his endearing charismatic style, Mark captures his audience's attention as well as their hearts. Having spoken to more than 6,000 audiences worldwide with his one-of-a-kind technique and masterful authority of his work, time and again he continues to receive high accolades from his listeners as one of the most dynamic and compelling speakers and leaders of our time.

Mark's credentials include a lifetime of entrepreneurial success and alternative energy pursuits, in addition to an extensive academic background. Many of his ideas about the comprehensive success of all humanity came from his years of undergraduate study with the famous Buckminster Fuller, one of Albert Einstein's greatest students.

Mark is also a prolific writer with many popular books such as the *Power of Focus, The Aladdin Factor, Dare to Win,* and *One Minute Millionaire,* which have inspired and helped thousands of people around the world to become millionaires. Mark has made a profound and positive influence through his extensive library of audio programs, video programs, and enriching articles in the areas of big thinking, sales achievement, publishing success, and personal and professional development.

Mark's energy and exuberance travels still further through mediums such as television *(Oprah, CNN* and *The Today Show),* print *(TIME, US News & World Report, USA Today, The New York Times* and *Entrepreneur)* and countless radio and newspaper interviews as he assures people everywhere that "With the right principles and mentors, you can easily create the life of your dreams."

He is also known as a passionate philanthropist and humanitarian, working tirelessly for organizations such as Habitat for Humanity, American Red Cross, March of Dimes, Childhelp USA, among others.

Mark serves as Chief Executive Officer of M.V. Hansen & Associates, Inc.; Cofounder of Chicken Soup for the Soul Enterprises, Inc.; President of One Minute Millionaire, LLC; and co-owner and founder of Natural Power Concepts.

Mark Victor Hansen is an enthusiastic crusader of what's possible and is driven to "make the world work for 100 percent of humanity."

Made in the USA
Monee, IL
29 June 2021